MW00774142

Ascent to Love

ASCENT TO LOVE

A Guide to Dante's Divine Comedy

PETER J. LEITHART

canonpress
Moscow, Idaho

Published by Canon Press
P.O. Box 8729, Moscow, ID 83843
800.488.2034 | www.canonpress.com

Peter J. Leithart, *Ascent to Love: A Guide to Dante's Divine Comedy*
Copyright © 2001 by Peter Leithart.

Cover design by David Dalbey.
Cover art: Gustave Doré (1832–1883), engravings from *The Divine Comedy*.

Printed in the United States of America.
All rights reserved. No part of this publication may be reproduced, stored in a
retrieval system, or transmitted in any form by any means, electronic, mechanical, photocopy, recording, or otherwise, without prior permission of the author,
except as provided by USA copyright law.

Library of Congress Cataloging-in-Publication Data

Leithart, Peter J.
  Ascent to love; a Guide to Dante's Divine Comedy / Peter J. Leithart.
  p. cm.
  Includes index.
 ISBN-13: 978-1-885767-16-5
 ISBN-10: 1-885767-16-1
  1. Dante Alighieri, 1265–1321. Divina commedia. I. Title.
 PQ4390 .L37 2001
                            2001001708

10 11 12 13 14 15 16   10 9 8 7 6 5

TO SHEFFIELD

Ecco chi crescera li nostri amori.
Paradiso 5.105

CONTENTS

ACKNOWLEDGMENTS

Ascent to Love is largely based on lectures that I have given in several settings. I first taught Dante several years ago to home school students in Birmingham, Alabama, as part of a course on medieval literature. For the past two years, I have taught the *Comedy* as part of my senior literature colloquium at New St. Andrews College. I have learned much from my students. During the summer of 2000, I lectured on Dante and medieval literature at a conference sponsored by the Covenant Classical School Association of Franklin, Tennessee. Thanks to George Grant and his cohorts for that invitation. Later in the summer, I presented much the same material at the Biblical Horizons conference in Niceville, Florida, at the request of James B. Jordan. Those two conferences forced me to formulate my thoughts about Dante in a compressed way, and I appreciate both opportunities. Doug Jones of Canon Press suggested that I write this book, and I am grateful, as usual, for his encouragement and generosity. Thanks are due, finally, to my son, Sheffield, who helped me get a head start by reformatting lecture notes into prose. During his last year of home schooling, I assigned the *Comedy* as part of Sheffield's reading in medieval literature, and, to put it mildly, Dante was not his favorite writer. When he learned that I was writing a book on Dante, he suggested the title *To Inferno and Beyond,* which I did not choose to use. Nonetheless, I hope he will not take my dedication of *Ascent to Love* to him as a mean-spirited joke, for it is done in all sincerity and love, and in the hope that Sheffield will always be a lover of the Love that moves the sun and all the other stars.

I HAVE COME TO THE GARDEN

The Classics, the Bible, and Love in Medieval Literature

Though Edmund Spenser was a contemporary of Shakespeare, he had at least one foot firmly planted in another age. His great sprawling poem, *The Faerie Queene*, was written in part to honor Queen Elizabeth I, but the poem is as medieval as anything the middle ages produced. Near the middle of Book 1, Redcrosse, the knight who will mature to become Saint George, the patron saint of Britain, is defeated and taken to the dungeon of Orgoglio, a giant. King Arthur shows up to rescue the beleaguered knight, but then he leaves. Redcrosse and his lady, Una, find themselves in the Cave of Despair, where Redcrosse is tempted to suicide. Una intervenes to save him and takes him to the House of Holiness, a kind of rehab center for backslidden knights, where three women, Faith, Hope, and Charity, nurse him back to physical and moral health.

Then he can continue the quest interrupted by his encounter with Orgoglio. He makes his way to a castle, where he fights a three-day battle with a dragon. On the first day, Redcrosse falls, but he is revived by water from the well of life; on the second day, he falls again, but he refreshes himself with fruit from the tree of life; but on the third day, Redcrosse defeats the dragon, and the wedding of Redcrosse and Una follows. No sooner has the celebration taken place than Redcrosse, like a modern superhero, is called back for another quest, another opportunity to save the world.

This story is so utterly medieval that it almost seems a parody of medieval literature. The characters and situations are obviously taken from medieval and Renaissance romance—the knights, the dragons, the ladies in distress, the escapes. In one fundamental way, however, Spenser parts company from medieval romance. To understand how radical Spenser is, however, we need to review some of the main features of Western medieval literature. Medieval literature takes its specific shape from the combination of three main factors: the pagan literature and stories of Greece, Rome, and Northern Europe; the Bible and interpretations of the Bible by the church fathers and medieval theologians; and the courtly love tradition that arose during the eleventh and twelfth centuries. When we have examined these, we shall be able to see the innovative direction of the *Faerie Queene*. We will also have the background to see how Dante's *Divine Comedy* is likewise both an heir to earlier medieval literature and at the same time something quite different.

Christendom and the Pagan Past

"Today," wrote the French playwright François Rabelais in his *Gargantua and Pantagruel*, "the old sciences are revived, knowledge is systematized, discipline re-established. The learned languages are restored: Greek, without which a man would be ashamed to consider himself educated; Hebrew, Chaldean, and Latin. Printing is now in use, an art so accurate and elegant that it betrays the divine inspiration of its discovery, which I have lived to witness. Alas! Conversely, I was not spared the horror of such diabolic works as gunpowder and artillery."[1]

Rabelais (1494–1553) was living through the latter part of the period known as the "Renaissance," and his character celebrates the achievements of his age with great optimism. For Rabelais and for many others, the Renaissance was the time when the lights were finally turned on, when the sun rose after a very long and very dark night.

Rabelais' view of the relation between the Renaissance and medieval world has been a popular one since his time, but recent

---

[1] Quoted by P.M. Pasinetti in Maynard Mack, ed., *World Masterpieces* (New York: W. W. Norton, 1974), 879.

1) stories of Greece, Rome, northern Europe ⎤
2) Bible   ⎬ medieval lit
3) courtly love   ⎦

I HAVE COME TO THE GARDEN   15

studies have shown that the line between them is blurry at best.

The name "Renaissance" refers to the rebirth of classical learning, but many classical writings and stories were known during the middle ages.[2] From the other direction, it has become clear that the Renaissance was full of superstition and occult interest; it was not the age of cool reason that textbooks often claim.[3] If the medieval world had some knowledge of ancient literature, however, they treated it with some care. Recognizing its pagan origins, they attempted to fit it into their Christian faith; when this could not be done, they cheerfully attacked and rejected it.

Conrad of Hirsau, a German schoolmaster of the eleventh and twelfth centuries, produced a work known as the *Dialogue on the Authors*, in which a pupil and teacher discuss the works of major pagan authorities. Overall, Conrad operates on the premise that "whatever truth and right thinking has ever been found in anyone has come from Him who created man," and he finds truth and right thinking in many pagan writers. Conrad, however, could also be withering in his scorn. He commended the Roman poet and satirist Horace because he provides "guidelines laid down for writing," but other parts of Horace are not so edifying, because his writing "is concerned with vice." Similarly, Conrad recommends a few works of Ovid, but condemns him as "the inventor of a large part of idol-worship in the *Metamorphoses*." Quoting Romans 1:18–23, he insists that Ovid's work is idolatrous because it is concerned with "the transformation of substances" and obscures "the faculty of reason in man, whereby he is made in the image and likeness of God."[4]

[2] See C.S. Lewis, *The Discarded Image: An Introduction to Medieval and Renaissance Literature* (Cambridge: Cambridge University Press, [1964] 1994).

[3] Frances A. Yates, *Giordano Bruno and the Hermetic Tradition* (Chicago: University of Chicago Press, 1964); Ioan P. Couliano, *Eros and Magic in the Renaissance*, trans. Margaret Cook (Chicago: University of Chicago Press, 1987); William Monter, *Ritual, Myth & Magic in Early Modern Europe* (Athens: Ohio University Press, 1983). Though it covers a later period, Keith Thomas's classic study, *Religion and the Decline of Magic* (New York: Scribner's, 1971), shows the persistence of magical beliefs and practices well past the beginning of the Renaissance.

[4] Quotations are from A.J. Minnis and A.B. Scott, eds., *Medieval Literary Theory and Criticism, c. 1100–c.1375: The Commentary Tradition* (Oxford: Clarendon, 1988), 56–58.

Though generally recognizing the sharp differences between pagan and Christian outlooks, medieval writers and commentators had different approaches to their classical and pagan inheritance. Though it is hardly an exhaustive classification, it is helpful to examine three of the ways that Christian writers dealt with the cultures of the past under the headings of "juxtaposition," "critique," and "incorporation."

Scholars debate whether *Beowulf* should be considered a Christian poem, but whether or not the characters are Christians, it is quite evident that the poet is. He writes of Cain, the Almighty, the Judge, the Creator. Within the story, the characters populate a heroic world that shares many customs and values with the world of Homer. When he is getting ready to dive into the water to fight Grendel's mother, Beowulf says, "As we must expect to leave our life on this earth, we must earn some renown, if we can, before death; daring is the thing for a fighting man to be remembered by"[5]—something that Achilles might have said in his most heroic moments. Later, the poet marvels at Beowulf's ferocity in battle: "A man must act so when he means in a fight to frame himself a long-lasting glory; it is not life he thinks of." Throughout the poem, pagan and Christian elements are side-by-side, juxtaposed, and the poet shows no recognition that there is a serious conflict between them.

A second option was to criticize the values and customs of ancient or Germanic heroes. Here the *Song of Roland*, the greatest of the *chasons de geste* ("songs of great deeds"), serves as an example. The poem tells of the battle of Roncevaux, a historical battle that occurred in 778 when Muslims attacked Charlemagne's army as he returned from a campaign against the Saracens in Northern Spain. Assisted by a Frankish traitor, Ganelon, the Muslims decimated the rear guard, which was under the command of Roland, Charlemagne's nephew and one of his Twelve Peers.

At the heart of the poem is the debate between Roland and his friend, Oliver, who urges Roland to blow his trumpet to call

---

[5] I am quoting the translation of Michael Alexander (London: Penguin, 1973).

reinforcements. Roland refuses until it is too late for Charlemagne, already far ahead, to help. The poem contrasts the foolish bravery of Roland with the wise prudence of Oliver. To be sure, Roland is no Achilles. More than anything, Achilles is out for personal glory, even if it means that he fights with his king and stands idly by watching his fellow warriors spill their blood before Hector's onslaught. A knight to the core, Roland knows he is a vassal, bound by oaths of loyalty to his king. Roland's glory is not so much the honor of personal achievement as the glory that he can bring to his lord. As he tells Oliver, "we must make a stand here for our king: one must endure hardships for one's lord and endure great heat and great cold, one must also lose hide and hair. Now let each see to it that he employ great blows, so that bad songs not be sung about us! I shall never be cited as a bad example."[6] Yet personal reputation is also important to Roland. He refuses to blow his horn because "in fair France my fame would suffer scorn." Calling for help would "cast dishonor on my house" and "on fair France bring ill renown." "Roland is fierce and Oliver is wise," says the poet, and Roland's heroic ferocity leads to utter disaster. Oliver rebukes his friend: "you got us into this mess. There is wise valour, and there is recklessness: Prudence is worth more than foolhardiness. Through your o'erweening you have destroyed the French." Though there is no indication that the poet of *Roland* knew anything of the classical world, the poem confronts head-on a key classical value—the hero's quest for personal honor.

Juxtaposition and critique are less common, however, than efforts to weave threads of Christian faith and the pagan past together into a single fabric. This method of "incorporation" could take one of two forms. On the one hand, Christian writers sometimes place their Christian stories within the larger framework of classical history or literature. The big story is the story of Troy or Greece or Rome, and the stories of the Christian world are chapters of that larger story. The delightful poem *Sir Gawaine and the Green Knight* is a tale of Arthur's court and of an Arthurian knight,

---

[6] I am using the translation of Dorothy L. Sayers, reprinted in Maynard Mack, ed., *World Masterpieces* (New York: W. W. Norton, 1974).

but it begins with a brief summary of the fall of Troy, Aeneas's journey to Italy, and the voyage of Aeneas's great-grandson, Felix Brutus, to Britain. The history of the Christian king Arthur thus continues a story that begins with the war on the windy plains of Troy, and Gawaine becomes a hero in the tradition of the Homeric heroes. Dante is doing something similar when he makes Virgil his guide through Hell and Purgatory, for he is presenting himself as a disciple and heir of the Roman poet. Moreover, as we shall see, at several points Dante compares himself to Aeneas, the hero of Virgil's epic.

In many cases, ancient heroes and events of classical history are placed within a Christian framework. At times this involves a shift from the emphasis of ancient literature to an emphasis more in keeping with Christian values.[7] During the middle ages, literary critics would introduce ancient texts with a summary of their contents and purpose; these introductory notes were known as *accessus ad auctores*. The *accessus* for the *Iliad* praises Homer for providing knowledge of the Trojan war and also because the "subject-matter is drawn from those who, as a result of an illicit union, caused the war." Homer's intention thus "is to dissuade anyone from such an illicit union, as a result of which he may incur the wrath of the gods, as did Paris, Helen, and the more courageous among their relatives who perished along with Troy in that war."[8] Though Homer certainly laments the waste of the Trojan War, no one reading the original poem would conclude that Homer meant it as a warning against adultery.

Medieval writers frequently resorted to ingenious allegorizations to incorporate pagan literature into a Christian worldview. An "allegorization" is a way of reading a story where the characters and events of the story are understood as symbols of ideas or moral principles. Augustine's interpretation of the parable of the Good Samaritan is a famous example of this method. According to Augustine, the man along the road represents the unsaved sinner; the

---

[7] Medieval treatments of Achilles provide a good example of this. For some details, see my *Heroes of the City of Man* (Moscow: Canon, 1999), 36–38.

[8] In Minnis and Scott, eds., *Medieval Literary Criticism*, 17.

Good Samaritan symbolizes Christ; the inn to which the Samaritan takes the wounded man is the church; and so on with every detail of the story. Medieval writers employed a similar method when they interpreted classical texts. Ovid's *Metamorphoses*, rejected with horror by Conrad of Hirsau, was seen by others as a mine of sacred truth and Christian morality. During the fourteenth century, an anonymous author (perhaps Philippe de Virtry, bishop of Meaux) wrote a long poem called *Ovid Moralise*, and other writers composed allegories of Ovid that were used for instruction of monks and nuns.[9]

Even pagan gods were kept alive during the middle ages, often by using the theory known as Euhemerism. Named for Euhemerus, a Greek poet of the third century B.C., this theory taught that the gods of the myths were once men, and their exploits were the exploits of ancient kings who later came to be treated as gods. Euhemerism was a pre-Christian method of interpreting ancient myths and was popular among sophisticated pagans seeking a more rational theology than Greek and Roman mythology provided.

Euhemerism had obvious attractions for early Christian writers. Clement of Alexandria, Lactantius, Tertullian, Augustine, and others all claimed that pagans were bowing before ancient men. While demoting the gods of the Greeks and Romans, Euhemerism simultaneously made ancient deities safe enough to be incorporated into a Christian account of history. If the gods and goddesses were just men and women, after all, then they were as historical as Adam, Noah, and Abraham, and Christian historians treated pagan gods as real historical figures. Eusebius claimed that Baal was the first king of Assyria, and that he lived at the time of the war of the Titans. Isidore of Seville's *Etymologies* attempts to place all the gods of the pagans in the various ages of history recounted in Scripture. The gods of Greece and Rome were often seen as sages

---

[9] Jean Seznec, *The Survival of the Pagan Gods: The Mythological Tradition and Its Place in Renaissance Humanism and Art,* trans. Barbara F. Sessions (New York: Harper Torchbook, 1961), 92.

who bequeathed to history various arts and sciences. According to the *Historia Scholastica* (A.D. 1160) of Peter Comestor, dean of Notre Dame at Troyes and later chancellor at Notre Dame, Minerva invented liberal arts, and Isis taught Egyptians the alphabet.[10]

In this respect, Spenser is as medieval as they come. The *Fairie Queene* is full of classical allusions, but they are all worked into a story and a religious outlook that is explicitly Christian. Similarly, in his use of pagan literature, Dante definitely practices "incorporation." Though pagan gods do not appear in the *Comedy*, many classical heroes and characters do, including Achilles, Ulysses, and some of the giants who rebelled against Zeus. And these classical figures are side-by-side with biblical characters and people from Dante's own time.

Review Questions

1. Was the Renaissance a complete break with the medieval world? Why or why not?

2. In what three ways did Christian writers use the literature and legends of the pagan past?

3. How is the *Song of Roland* a critique of the ancient heroic ideal?

4. Why is it significant that *Sir Gawaine and the Green Knight* begins with the history of Troy?

5. What is allegorization? How was it used to interpret pagan literature?

6. What is Euhemerism?

The Book of Books

Though medieval writers used pagan and classical literature in various ways, the book that formed the foundation of medieval society was the Bible. From the time of Origen and Augustine,

---

[10] For more, see ibid.

every area of study was important because it could shed light on the biblical text. Monasteries, centers of medieval intellectual and cultural life, were devoted to copying Scripture, copying commentaries on Scripture, chanting Scripture, commenting on Scripture, meditating on Scripture.

Medieval political life was likewise infused with Scripture. Few statements of political theory have had as much impact on the development of Western institutions as that of Pope Gelasius: "Two there are, August Emperor, by which this world is ruled on title of original and sovereign grant—the consecrated authority of the priesthood and the royal power."[11] Gelasius was emphasizing that God had established not only the state but the church as a ruler on earth, and he was claiming that the church had an equal role to play in the government of the world. Some of the most important political battles of the middle ages were struggles over the meaning of this principle. Strikingly, this fundamental political axiom occurs in the midst of the Pope's discussion of the typological connections between Melchizedek and Jesus. In other words, the whole balance of power between pope and emperor was founded on a piece of biblical interpretation. Political rituals, such as anointing and investiture, were also drawn from Scripture.[12] When Charlemagne was anointed by the Pope in 800, he not only became the reborn "Roman" Emperor but began to think of himself as a new David, ruling over a "new Israel."

Medieval writers interpreted the Bible through the grid of the "fourfold sense" of Scripture. Though not the first to discuss issues

[11] Quoted in George Weigel, *Tranquillitas Ordinis: The Present Failure and Future Promise of American Catholic Thought on War and Peace* (Oxford: Oxford University Press, 1987). The Gelasian formula was as important to medieval political life as "All men are created equal" is in modern politics. For more on the Bible in medieval political theory, see Walter Ullmann, *A History of Political Thought: The Middle Ages* (Baltimore: Penguin, 1965); Ullmann, *Principles of Government and Politics in the Middle Ages* (London: Methuen, 1961).

[12] See the fascinating study of Ernst H. Kantorowicz, *The King's Two Bodies: A Study in Medieval Political Theology* (Princeton: Princeton University Press, 1957); and Johan Chydenius, *Medieval Institutions and the Old Testament* (Societas Scientiarum Fennica, Commentationes Humanarum Litterarum, 37.2; Helsinki: Helsingfors, 1965).

of interpretation in this way, John Cassian gave classic expression to this method. The theory is that each story, event, person, or institution in Scripture can be interpreted in four different senses. The first is the literal or historical sense; interpreted in this way, a biblical text literally states who did what where. Especially in the Old Testament, events of history are symbolic of things that are yet to come. Thus, each event points to the work of Christ and the life of the church. There is also an "eschatological" dimension to every text of Scripture, pointing to the final consummation of all things in a new heavens and new earth. Finally, every text has an application to the individual Christian life. As it was summarized in a brief lyric:

> Littera gesta docet, quid credas allegoria,
> Moralis quid agas, quo tendas anagogia.[13]

Which, roughly translated, means,

> The literal teaches past deeds, the allegorical what you are to believe,
> The moral [tropological] what you are to do, the anagogical what you hope to achieve.

Cassian offered the example of the city of Jerusalem. Interpreted historically or literally (*secundum historiam*), Jerusalem is the capital city of Israel from the time of David, the city in which Jesus was crucified. Allegorically, the historical city points ahead to the "new Jerusalem," the church (*secundum allegoriam*). Though the church is already the new Jerusalem, the church has not yet reached its final destination, and therefore passages about "Jerusalem" also point ahead to the heavenly city. This is called the "anagogical" sense (*secundum anagogiam*). Finally, tropologically, the history of Jerusalem can be understood as a model for the history of the soul (*secundum tropologiam*).[14] Just as David conquered Jerusalem

---

[13] Quoted by A. J. Minnis, *Medieval Theory of Authorship: Scholastic Literary Attitudes in the Later Middle Ages* (London: Scholar Press, 1984), 34.

[14] The classic work on medieval exegesis is the four-volume study of Henri de Lubac, *Exegese medievale*, now happily being published in English by Eerdmans under the title *Medieval Exegesis*. Volumes 1 and 2 have now been published. *Tolle, lege.*

and set up the Lord's throne there, so Jesus, His Son, conquers the inner city of the sinner and consecrates him as a saint, a holy one. Another classic and frequent example is the Song of Songs,[15] which can be interpreted in each of the four modes. Historically, it refers (so medievals often said) to the love between King Solomon and the daughter of Pharaoh. Allegorically, it refers to the love between Christ and His church. Anagogically, it is a poem about the resurrection and the final marriage supper of the lamb, and tropologically, it celebrates the soul's "marriage" with her beloved.

Without denying the historicity of any of the events recounted in Scripture, medieval writers also insisted that Scripture has a richness and fullness of meaning; not a bare record of historical events. Everything in Scripture points forward (horizontally, historically) and upward (as an image of heaven); it speaks not only of the universe as a whole, the macrocosm (allegorical/anagogical), but also of the human soul, the microcosm (tropological).

Medieval literature overflows with examples of this method of interpretation. William Langland's fourteenth-century work, *Piers the Plowman,* is a dream allegory similar to Dante and Milton in some ways, but more like *Pilgrim's Progress* in others. One example from this work will illustrate the influence not only of the Bible but of the Bible interpreted through the tradition of patristic exegesis. Defending the superiority of a life of holy poverty, Langland refers to the incident with Mary and Martha in Luke's gospel and concludes that Jesus "put poverty first and praised it the more highly." He goes on: "And as far as I can discover, all the wise men of the past have praised poverty, and said that, borne with patience, it is the best life—many times more blessed than riches. For although it is bitter to the taste, there comes sweetness afterwards; and just

[15] Mary Dove points out that the very name, *Canticum canticorum,* points to its supremacy as *the* medieval "Book of Love" (Dove, "'Swiche Olde Lewed Wordes,': Books About Medieval Love, Medieval Books About Love, and the Medieval Book of Love," in Andrew Lynch and Philippa Maddern, eds., *Venus and Mars: Engendering Love and War in Medieval and Early Modern Europe* (Nedlands: University of Western Australia Press, 1995), 21. See also E. Ann Matter, *The Voice of My Beloved: The Song of Songs in Western Medieval Christianity* (Philadelphia: University of Pennsylvania Press, 1990).

as a walnut has a bitter shell, but when the shell is removed there is
a kernel of strengthening food, so it is with poverty and mortifica-
tion when taken patiently. Poverty makes a man mindful of God,
and gives him a strong desire to pray well and weep for his sins; and
from these things Mercy arises, of which the kernel is Christ, who
comforts and strengthens the soul."[16]

The "nut of poverty" image seems a quaint piece of allegory,
but behind Langland is a long tradition of interpreting Song of
Songs 6:11 ("I went down to the orchard of nut trees"). Earlier
commentators on the Song of Songs focused on the hardness and
bitterness of the nut's shell in contrast to the sweetness of the inside
fruit. From this, commentators frequently moved to a meditation
on the role of chastisement, which seems bitter but produces sweet
fruit for those who endure it. Another line of interpretation linked
the nut to Christ's two natures: The hard and unattractive shell is
the human nature of Christ, within which is hidden the sweetness
of divinity. Alternatively, the shell is interpreted as the sufferings
of Christ, again as a veil for the divinity behind. Langland subtly
merges the two senses within so that the shell becomes the symbol
both of the hardness of life in poverty and a sign of Christ's sufferings. The implication is that enduring the hard shell of suffering is a
way of taking up one's cross in union with Christ. The sweetness of
poverty is thus not that it develops character in some general sense,
but specifically that it deepens one's knowledge of Christ.

Langland was a cleric writing a spiritual allegory, but even
"secular" writers of the middle ages, such as Chaucer, were thoroughly at home in the world of biblical imagery. According to one
scholar's tally, "there are more than eighty explicit references to
Paul and his Epistles in *The Canterbury Tales* and numerous exten-
sions of Pauline imagery and spiritual concerns."[17] The "Wife of
Bath's Tale" is full of allusions to Paul's discussion of marriage and

---

[16] I am using the translation of J.F. Goodridge (New York: Penguin, 1966).

[17] Russell A. Peck, "Biblical Interpretation: St. Paul and *The Canterbury Tales*," in
David Lyle Jeffrey, ed., *Chaucer and Scriptural Tradition* (Ottawa: University of Ottawa
Press, 1984).

celibacy in 1 Corinthians 7.[18] In her case, this quotation is highly ironic; the whole passage in 1 Corinthians is an exhortation to self-control, but the woman who quotes the passage has had five husbands and is quite free sexually. Chaucer's biblical quotations are sometimes partial, but deliberately so. In the *"Summoner's Tale,"* Friar John quotes half the beatitude "Blessed are the poor in spirit" but does not mention the second half, which promises that the reward for the poor in spirit is the kingdom of heaven. Such a partial quotation is self-serving for the greedy John, who wants his rewards here and now, not in heaven.[19]

In the "General Prologue," Chaucer describes his summoner (a constable who summons accused persons to court) as a man who loves "garlic, onions, leeks." This refers to Israel in the wilderness complaining that they no longer ate the leeks and garlics of Egypt (Num. 11:5). In a sermon on this text, Gregory the Great, bishop of Rome in the sixth century, expounded the Numbers passage by pointing out that leeks and onions cause tears. Such tears, however, are not the result of true repentance, but represent merely the sorrows of the world; they are tears shed by people who refuse to leave the leeks and onions of Egypt behind. Ironically, Gregory goes on to say, they refuse the good food of manna in favor of food that aggravates their condition, and thus they end up striving to get the food that causes them pain. In this brief allusion to the Summoner's diet, Chaucer has offered an important clue to the man's character.

Chaucer's bawdy tales include many allusions to the Song of Songs, but mostly as parodies of the biblical poem. In the "Miller's Tale," the lover Absolon comes to the window of Alisoun, pining in love for her:

Where are you, honeycomb, sweet Alisoun?
My sweetest cinnamon, my pretty chick?
Awake and speak to me, sweetheart, awake!

[18] For details, see Lawrence Besserman, *Chaucer's Biblical Poetics* (Norman: University of Oklahoma Press, 1998), 106.

[19] See the discussion in ibid., 101.

It's little thought that you give to my sorrow,
Or what a sweat I'm in for love of you;
For it's no wonder that I swoon and sweat,
I'm yearning like a lambkin for the teat.
Truly, sweetheart, I am so much in love,
I yearn for you like any turtle-dove
After its mate; I eat less than a girl.[20]

Absolon's words are a collection of texts from the Song of Songs.
Calling Alisoun a "honeycomb" draws on "Your lips, my bride, drip
honey; honey and milk are under your tongue" (4:11). According
to the biblical poet, within the garden that is the beloved are scents
of "Nard and saffron, calamus and cinnamon, with all the trees of
frankincense" (4:14). In the Song of Songs, when the lover calls,
the bride says, "I was asleep, but my heart was awake. A voice! My
beloved was knocking: 'Open to me, my sister, my darling, my
dove, my perfect one,'" (5:2). She rises from bed to go to him: "my
hands dripped with myrrh, and my fingers with liquid myrrh, on
the handles of the bolt." But when she opens to the beloved, she
finds he "had turned away and had gone . . . . I searched for him,
but I did not find him; I called him, but he did not answer me"
(5:5–6).

In Chaucer's parody, however, Absolon's approaches do not
receive so welcoming a response:

"Go from the window, jackanapes," said [Alisoun],
"No kiss-me-quick for you—God save us all!
I love another—and small blame to me—
Better than you, by Jesus, Absolon!
Be off with you now, or I'll throw a stone,
Go in the devil's name, and let me sleep!"

In the end, Alisoun agrees to let Absolon kiss her, but the method
she uses must remain unwritten, this being a family book and all.

---

[20] I am using the translation of David Wright (World Classics; Oxford: Oxford University Press, 1986). Chaucer is also satirizing the conventions of courtly love poetry.

Perhaps the most common biblical setting that appears in medieval literature and art is the garden. Throughout the *Canterbury Tales*, lovely women appear, like new Eves, in gardens. In the "Knight's Tale," Chaucer describes the lovely Emily:

> So time passed, year by year and day by day,
> Till it so happened, in the month of May,
> That Emily, lovelier to look upon
> Than is the lily on the stalk of green,
> And fresher than the May with flowers new—
> For with the rose's colour strove her hue,
> Nor can I tell the lovelier of the two—
> Well before day, as she was wont to do,
> Was risen and dressed and ready to go out,
> For, as you know, the nights are not for sleep
> In May.

Emily is first seen in a garden in springtime, but she is not merely *in* the garden; she becomes the loveliest flower of the garden, an incarnation of the season itself. Palamon and Arcita, seeing Emily from their prison window, are seeing an Edenic world to which they have no access.

"The Merchant's Tale" plays with the garden-bride connection in a different way. The elderly January is married to lusty young May. To please her, he builds a "garden walled about with stone," and he

> Took such delight in walking in this garden
> He wouldn't trust the key to anyone
> Except himself; he carried in his pocket
> A silver latchkey to unlock the wicket
> —The little garden-gate—at his good pleasure.
> And when he wished to pay his wife her due
> He would go thither in the summer weather

> With May his wife, and not one but they two.
> And all those things which were not done in bed,
> He in the garden with advantage did.
> And in this manner many a happy day
> Old January passed with lovely May.

The garden here becomes a garden of earthly delights, and January's exclusive claim to his bride is symbolized by his exclusive access to his garden. As the story progresses, both the garden and the bride are violated when May makes a copy of the key for a younger and more attractive lover, Damian.

Another use of garden imagery appears in Boccaccio's *Decameron*. The "frame story" tells about a group of young men and women who escape from plague-ridden Florence to wait out the plague in a country villa. To pass the time, they tell stories each day, stories that are often sexually explicit. On the third day of their retreat, the storytellers move to a second location, where there is a garden, an earthly paradise. It is a secular recovery of Eden, where men and women speak nakedly and are not ashamed.

Again, the two poets with which we began—Spenser and Dante—are thoroughly medieval in their interest in biblical imagery. Spenser, after all, is not just writing an adventure story, but a moral and theological allegory, and biblical imagery suffuses the whole story. In the final scenes, Redcrosse becomes a Christ figure who slays the great dragon on the third day, as well as a Christian, sustained in battle by water and food, by baptism and communion. In these respects too, Spenser's poem is a relic of an earlier period. Dante, as we shall see throughout this book, refers to many biblical stories and characters; he is quite at home employing the notion of the "fourfold sense."

Thus far, we have not isolated what separates Spenser from the medieval tradition, or what separates him from Dante. Both questions can be answered after we have examined the medieval conception of love, which is the subject of the next section.

Review Questions

1. What is the "fourfold sense" of Scripture? Give an example.
2. How does Chaucer use scriptural quotations in his poetry?
3. Explain how Chaucer is using the Song of Songs in "The Miller's Tale."
4. Give some examples of how medieval writers used the "garden" theme.

Source of All Good Things

No less an authority than C.S. Lewis called the rise of the courtly love tradition in eleventh-century France a "real change in human sentiment," which "has left no corner of our ethics, our imagination, or our daily life untouched." Courtly love poets "erected impossible barriers between us and the classical past or the Oriental present. Compared with this revolution, the Renaissance is a mere ripple on the surface of literature."[21] The ideals of courtly love persist to this day. Denis de Rougemont has suggested that since the eleventh century, "love" and especially "falling in love" have meant something quite different from what they meant at any previous time in history. For both the late medieval courtier and the modern romantic, "love" means this kind of love, the conventions of courtly love.[22]

"Courtly love," a phrase that first appeared in an article by Gaston Paris published in the 1880s, does not describe a particular type or genre of literature but a particular view of love, which may be manifested in a number of different genres. Themes of courtly love begin to appear in the lyric poetry of the "troubadours" in the Provence and Languedoc regions of southwestern France in the eleventh century. Traveling poets and singers, the troubadours created the first important body of vernacular poetry in the Western

---

[21] C.S. Lewis, *The Allegory of Love: A Study in Medieval Tradition* (Oxford: Oxford University Press, 1936), 4, 11.

[22] Denis de Rougemont, *Love in the Western World*, trans. by Montgomery Belgion (Princeton: Princeton University Press, 1983).

world, that is, poetry that is written in the common language of the people rather than in Greek or Latin. Similar themes are found in later "chivalric romances," the stories of love and adventure, of dashing knights and damsels in distress that we think of as typically medieval. By the late twelfth century, the courtly love tradition was established well enough to be codified in Andre Campellanus's treatise on *The Art of Courtly Love*.[23] Courtly love themes are evident in a religious guise in allegorical poetry and the writings of mystics such as Bernard of Clairvaux.

With regard to timing and location, the genesis of this tradition is specific and well known. Explaining where the courtly love tradition came from, and why it came into being at all, is much more difficult. It is certainly not a product of the ancient world. As Lewis says, "In ancient literature love seldom arises above the levels of merry sensuality or domestic comfort, except to be treated as a tragic madness, an ατη which plunges otherwise sane people, usually women, into crime and disgrace"—women such as Virgil's Dido or Euripides' Medea or Phaedra. The love of Odysseus for Penelope is more typical, not to mention much safer: He "loves Penelope as he loves the rest of his home and possessions."[24] Since the passion was considered dangerous, it was feared and avoided.

Even Ovid, the great ancient writer on love, did not think of love in the same way as the troubadours. He treats romantic love with mock seriousness, and ancient readers would probably have gotten the joke. Advising the young lover, for example, Ovid writes:

> Go early ere th' appointed hour to meet
> The fair, and long await her in the street.
> Through shouldering crowds on all her errands run,
> Though graver business wait the while undone.
> If she commands your presence on her way

---

[23] See the brief overview of the stages of development in Heather M. Arden, *The Romance of the Rose* (Boston: Twayne, 1987), 21–28.

[24] Lewis, *Allegory of Love*, 4.

Home from the ball to lackey her, obey!
Or if from rural scenes she bids you, "Come,"
Drive if you can, if not, then walk, to Rome.
And let nor Dog-star nor drifted load
Of whitening snows deter you from the road.
Cowards, fly hence! Our general, Love, disdains
Your lukewarm service in his long campaign.[25]

Some of this advice is found in courtly love poetry, but the medievals appear to take it with high seriousness. As Lewis says, the
courtly love tradition is partly a matter of "Ovid misunderstood,"
as medieval poets took his sardonic advice as sound instruction
for lovers.

If the courtly love tradition did not arise from ancient patterns
of sentiment, it did not arise from Christianity either, at least not in
any direct way. Love, to be sure, has a higher profile in the thought
and writing of the early Christians than it did in the ancient world,
largely for theological reasons. Ancient mythologies included love
as a god, as Ovid does in his parodic way, but no ancient thinker
or poet anticipated John's claim that "God is Love." Nor would the
ancients have defined the love that is God in the way the Bible does,
as God's self-giving sacrifice for the salvation of His people. With
its emphasis on the supremacy of charity in theology and ethics,
Christianity was a necessary condition for the rise of courtly love.

But it was not a sufficient condition. Early medieval poetry,
though Christian, shows no sign of interest in romantic love of
this kind. *Beowulf* takes place in a world of men, and the hero does
not take his cues from a lady. Roland is not fighting for his fiance
back in France, but out of obligation to his liege and for the sake of
the honor he hopes to win in France. When "love" is used in these
poems, it more often refers to the vassal's utter loyalty to his lord
than to romantic love. Written two centuries before the troubadours
appeared, the poetry of the Carolingian Renaissance deals with
politics, theology, current events, Scripture, and many other topics.
Love is an important element in the poetry, but, as Peter Godman

[25] *Art of Love* 2.223, quoted in ibid., 7.

observes, it is "divine love." By contrast, "of human love there is
hardly a trace and of romantic sentiment there is nothing at all."[26]
Against the idea that Christianity provided the direct and immedi-
ate inspiration for courtly love stands the brute fact of chronology.
Europe had been predominantly Christian for more than half a
millennium before the troubadours sang their first song. If it is a
Christian form of poetry, why the delay?[27]

Some scholars have suggested that courtly love arises in particular social circumstances. Lewis points out that medieval marriages
were more for business than pleasure. Marriage was a way of uniting
feuding families, or of maintaining property and title. Romance, if
it was to be found at all, had to be found outside marriage. Howard
Bloch concludes that the increasing ability of women to dispose
of property provoked a shift in men's attitudes toward them. Men
became more openly complimentary when they realized that they
could make a fortune by winning the favor of a wealthy lady. Others
have emphasized the specific location where the troubadours first
appeared. Provence and Languedoc were close to Muslim Spain,
and it is possible that the troubadours were influenced by Arabic love
poetry from that region. Further, Languedoc was a hotbed of heretical Catharism, and de Rougemont has suggested that the courtly
love tradition is a veiled form of heretical mysticism.[28] Though few
have endorsed the specifics of de Rougemont's account, his notion
that courtly love represents a development within Christian heresy

[26] Peter Godman, *Poetry of the Carolingian Renaissance* (Norman: University of
Oklahoma Press, 1985), 76. The one exception is the late Carolingian epic-like *Waltharius*,
which Godman compares to the romances of the eleventh century (p. 76).

[27] R. Howard Bloch has recently suggested that the courtly love tradition is simply a
new twist on the early Christian "obsession" with virginity and chastity. Rather than being
a break with the tradition of Christian "misogyny" and the beginning of a new respect for
women, courtly love is a "moment" in the history of misogyny: "the debilitating obsession
with woman as the source of all evil became inverted into a co-conspiring obsession with
woman as the source of all good" (*Medieval Misogyny and the Invention of Western Romantic
Love* [Chicago: University of Chicago Press, 1991], 11).

[28] de Rougemont, *Love in the Western World*, Books II–III. For an intriguing account
of the culture of Languedoc during this period, see Emmanuel Le Roy Ladurie, *Montaillou:
The Promised Land of Error* (New York: Vintage Books, 1979).

is attractive, for reasons to be mentioned again below.

But enough of origins. Wherever it came from, courtly love came. But what was it?[29] First, the love celebrated in courtly love lyrics and romances is often illicit and even adulterous. Lewis, in fact, lists adultery as one of the key features of the courtly love tradition. This is not to say that adultery was acceptable socially, and the poems and romances themselves often condemn adultery. But in courtly love literature the love is unacceptable in some way. Among the most famous of medieval romances was the story of Tristan and Isolde.[30] Tristan is nephew and knight of King Mark of Cornwall. As a trusted vassal, he is sent to fetch the beautiful Isolde, princess of Ireland, who has been engaged to Mark. As Tristan and Isolde prepare to leave Ireland, Isolde's mother gives her maidservant a bottle of love potion for Mark and Isolde to take on their wedding night. Along the way home—of course—both Tristan and Isolde inadvertently drink from the potion and fall madly in love. Isolde marries Mark, but she changes places with her maidservant on their wedding night because she wants to be true to Tristan.

Throughout the story, the lovers are torn between loyalty to Mark and their love for one another, but in general their love wins out. They take every possible opportunity to meet secretly, evading detection by various ruses and deceptions. Isolde is even able to pass a trial by ordeal and "prove" her innocence. Knowing that the ordeal is coming, she arranges for Tristan to meet her ship at the shore, disguised as a traveler. When Isolde attempts to disembark from the boat, the "traveler" carries her to dry land. Later, during the trial by ordeal, she is asked whether she has ever been in any man's

---

[29] A helpful compendium of sources may be found in Lewis Freeman Mott, *The System of Courtly Love, Studied as an Introduction to the Vita Nuova of Dante* (New York: Haskell House, 1965). This book must be used carefully, however, since Mott's quotations are listed without context.

[30] There are a number of different versions of the story. I am summarizing the story as told by Gottfried von Strassburg, as translated in Roger Sherman Loomis and Laura Hibbard Loomis, eds., *Medieval Romances* (New York: Modern Library, 1957).

arms other than her husband's, and she laughingly replies that she has been only in the arms of her husband—and the traveler who carried her to shore a few days before.

In the end, Tristan cannot go on with his divided life, and he returns to his homeland, where he marries another woman named "Isolde." Injured while helping another man seduce a married woman, Tristan sends a ship back to Cornwall to beg the original Isolde to nurse him back to health, which she has done before. He tells the captain of the ship to put up a flag to announce whether Isolde has returned or not. If she is on board the ship, the flag should be white, while a black flag is a sign that she has refused to come. Isolde does return at Tristan's call, but Tristan's wife, understandably jealous after years of dwelling in the suburbs of her husband's affections, tells Tristan that the flag is black. Tristan dies of grief, and by the time Isolde comes ashore the funeral is already in progress. She climbs into Tristan's bier and dies with him, and they are buried side by side. A vine and rose bush are planted atop their graves, which intertwine as they grow.

The lady in a romance is not always married, but she is always inaccessible for some reason or another—because of family conflicts (as in *Romeo and Juliet*), a domineering father (as in *Taming of the Shrew*), or because of her too-high or too-low social status (as in *Pride and Prejudice*, though Austen's lovers are hardly courtly lovers). The hopeless situation gives a particular shading to the lover's love and to his love poetry. Courtly love poetry is full of sighs, tears, lamentation, and sorrow. For the courtly lover, love is a sickness, a wound; it leaves the lover sleepless, without appetite, full of sighs, his face pallorous. When Tristan and Isolde drink of the love potion, their hearts are joined together in both love and sorrow, and Tristan particularly feels "pangs of Love." As de Rougemont points out, courtly lovers revel in obstacles, for obstacles keep the passion aflame. This combination of sorrow and pleasure is one of the most characteristic features of this poetry, and of Western love poetry in general. A lyric from one of the most famous of the troubadours,

Arnaut Daniel,[31] illustrates the point. In *"En cest sonet coind'e leri,"* he speaks of his love-sickness:

> I do not want the empire of Rome,
> do not make me pope of it
> so that I could not turn back to her
> for whom the heart in me burns and breaks apart.
> If she does not kiss me before new year's,
> she murders me and sends herself to hell.
> But this torment I endure
> could not make me turn away from loving well,
> though it holds me fast in loneliness,
> for in this desert I cast my words in rhyme.
> I labor in loving more than a man who works the earth,
> for the Lord of Moncli did not love
> N'audierna an egg's worth more.

Andre Campellanus, codifier of the tradition, knew his sources well, for he defined love as "a certain inborn suffering derived from the sight of and excessive meditation upon the beauty of the opposite sex."[32]

In romances, these same obstacles provide much of the drama of the story. Because they must meet in secret, steal a few moments together, and always under the threat of being found out, the lovers' trysts are exciting and daring. What keeps the passion passionate is that it is not consummated, or that it is consummated rarely and secretly. The lover's heroics are shown in his endurance of the anguish of unfulfilled love.

Viewed from this angle, de Rougemont's claim that the courtly

---

[31] Daniel was a troubadour of the late twelfth century. He appears in *Purgatory*, canto 26, among those who are being purged of lust, and speaks to Dante in Provencal, the only non-Italian to speak his native tongue in the whole of the *Comedy*. The phrase that begins his final plea to Dante is "Ara vos prec," "I beg you," as he asks Dante to remember him when he leaves Purgatory. Largely through Dante's influence, Daniel's notoriety continued into this century; T.S. Eliot's 1920 collection of poems bore the original title, *Ara vos prec*.

[32] Quoted in Maxwell Luria, *A Reader's Guide to the Roman de la Rose* (Hamden: Archon Books, 1982), 175.

love tradition arises from Christian heresies gains considerable plausibility. The story line of the courtly love lyric or romance is that a man devotes himself entirely to the service and salvation of a lady, and it is hard to think about this without recognizing some similarities with the gospel announcement that the Son of God has endured suffering and death for the sake of His bride. So far, so good. But courtly love never comes to consummation; the courtly romance does not end in covenant and marriage, a permanent bond of love and loyalty. Instead, it ends with death and separation, or, as in Tristan and Isolde's case, with union in death. De Rougemont suggests that the courtly love tradition arises from a death wish. That is perhaps going too far, but there is clearly a strong sense of the tragic potential of love. What in the Christian gospel is a comedy of salvation ending with a wedding becomes in the courtly love tradition a tragedy ending with a (double) funeral.[33]

Accompanying this tragic sentiment is an idealization of the lady. These two features of courtly love are necessary to one another. If the lover were to get close enough to his beloved to actually *know* her, live with her, and be married to her, he would soon discover flaws both in her beauty and her character. From a distance, the lover cannot see her blemishes, and he therefore considers her the jewel that all the world cannot afford to buy, the sun, the stars, the world. Arnaut serves "the noblest lady in the world" and the lover of the *Romance of the Rose* sees among the many roses one "so beautiful that in comparison none of its mates I prized at all" (7.35–37).[34]

Some have suggested that the courtly love tradition involves the "feudalization of love." There is something to this, for if the lady responds favorably to the lover, they are bound by oaths of

[33] I owe this suggestion to my friend, Rich Bledsoe, pastor of Tree of Life Presbyterian Church, Boulder, Colorado.

[34] Bloch's counterintuitive argument that courtly love draws on the traditional Christian emphasis on the superiority of virginity becomes plausible in this context. Though concerned with romantic love, and sometimes overtly sexual, courtly love poetry always keeps the object of love at a distance. If the lady were not pure, she would not be desirable. Thus, the courtly lover paradoxically longs for a consummated love with a woman whom he will love only so long as she remains a virgin. In Bloch's own words: "the sine qua non of

fealty. The lover must do the bidding of the lady in such a way that the lady takes the place of the feudal Lord. In the same lyric quoted above, Arnaut declares,

> Each day I am a better man and purer,
> for I serve the noblest lady in the world,
> and I worship her, I tell you this in the open.
> I belong to her from my foot to the top of my head;
> and let the cold wind blow,
> love raining in my heart
> keeps me warm when it winters most.

The lover's fidelity to the lady overrides all other loyalties. Tristan feels conflict between his desire for honor, his duty toward King Mark, and his love for Isolde. But his love for Isolde constantly wins out, and he ends up being deceptive, manipulative, and a traitor to his lord. In this respect, the courtly love tradition is very much alive. For Hollywood, a real love is one that so transcends all other loyalties that everything else falls into the background. The recent Oscar-winning film *The English Patient* is set against the background of World War II, but the war plays so small a role that we almost forget it is going on at all. What is important, what is *all*-important, is the consuming passion of the (adulterous) lovers. Saving the world from Nazi totalitarianism fades to nothing by comparison.

In medieval literature, love takes on religious dimensions as the Lady becomes an object not merely of chivalric loyalty and feudal fidelity, but of worship. "Hands joined, head bowed, I give and commend myself to you," writes the early troubadour Bernart de Ventadorn. Chretien de Troies, one of the great medieval writers of romance, describes Lancelot's devotion to his queen and lady:

---

desire—that is, of a woman's being loved—is that she be perfect. Yet the condition of her perfection is that she be self-sufficient, self-contained, complete—or that, being desired, she herself should not desire. . . . The perfection of the love object excludes or prevents her desiring. To be loved, according to the logic of the courtly relation, the woman must be indifferent, unattainable, unsullied—in short, a virgin" (*Medieval Misogyny*, 147).

"He adores her and bows down to her, for in no holy body does he so believe." "If in belief I were so faithful to God," another poet opines, "without fail I should enter Paradise alive." Peire Vidal's worship is more overtly sensual: "Good lady, I think I see God when I gaze upon your tender body."[35]

The greatest and most influential work of the French middle ages, the *Romance of the Rose*, provides an expanded example of how all these themes of courtly love are woven together in a single poem. The *Romance* was written in two unequal parts by two different authors, the first 4000 lines by Guillaume de Lorris around 1237, and the last 21,780 lines by Jean de Meun forty years later. An allegorical dream vision, the Romance tells the story of a man who comes upon a walled garden, which, he discovers, belongs to Mirth. After some unsuccessful attempts to scale the wall, he gains entry with the help of a lovely young lady named "Idleness." After meeting Mirth and others, he begins to explore the garden, all the while pursued by the God of Love, who has five arrows at the ready. At the center of the garden, the dreamer finds the reflecting pool in which Narcissus drowned, from which he can see reflections of all the plants of the garden. There, reflected on the jewels at the bottom of the pool, he spies a rose bud far lovelier than all others, though the bush is surrounded by a hedge of thorns. Having chosen to devote himself to this rose, the God of Love shoots arrows at him that go through his eye and into his heart. He has received the "wound of love," and he spends the rest of the poem trying to win the affection of the rose and gain a kiss.

After the God of Love has wounded the lover, he draws near and initiates a feudal ceremony that binds the lover as a vassal to Love:[36]

---

[35] All the quotations in this paragraph are from Mott, *System of Courtly Love*, 13, 40, 91.

[36] I am using the translation of Harry W. Robbins (New York: E. P. Dutton, 1962).

"Vassal, you now are seized; there's nothing here
To aid you in defense or toward escape.
In giving yourself up make no delay;
For the more willingly you abdicate
That much more quickly will you mercy gain.
He is a fool who with refusal thwarts
The one whom he should coax and supplicate.
Against my power no striving will avail.
Be well advised by me that foolish pride
Will gain you nothing; cede yourself as thrall
Calmly and with good grace, as I desire."
I answered simply, "Sire, to you I give
Myself most willingly; nor will I strive
To make resistance to your will. Please God
That I rebellious thoughts may never have
Against your rule. 'Twere neither just nor right.
Do what you please with me: or hand or slay.
My life is in your hands. I cannot swerve.
I cannot live a day against your will.
By you to weal and welfare I might mount
That by no other could I gain. Your hand,
Which thus has wounded me, must give me cure;
Make me your prisoner. I'll feel no ire
So long as I am saved from your disdain.
Of you so much that's good I've heard men say
That 'tis my wish to yield myself to you,
Completely in your service then to be,
Body and soul. If I perform your will,
Nothing can give me grief. But, furthermore,
I hope that at some time I may have grace
To gain that which I now so much desire.
I yield myself upon this covenant."

(*Romance* 8.151–182)

As lord by covenant, the God of Love then announces to the
lover the commandments of love. Among these is this instruction:

> In ladies' service labor and take pains;
> Honor and champion them; and if you hear
> Calumnious or spiteful talk of them
> Reprove the speaker; bid him hold his tongue.
> Do what you can damsels and dames to please.
> <div align="right">(<i>Romance</i> 9.82–86)</div>

Echoes of Ovid are evident here, but this time Ovid is in earnest.

Serving the God of Love and devotion to the service of a lady
means hardship and suffering. As the God of Love explains, "When,
as my sermoning advises you, Your heart you have bestowed, there
will befall adventures hard and heavy for Love's thane" (10.1–3).
The lover will be forced to withdraw from company to avoid detection, and

> Then in your loneliness will come to you
> Sighs and complaints, tremors and other ills.
> Tormented will you be in many ways:
> One hour you will be hot, another cold;
> One hour you will be flushed, another pale;
> No quartan fever that you have had—
> Nor quotidian either—could be worse.
> The Pains of Love you will experience
> Ere you recover thence.
> <div align="right">(<i>Romance</i> 10.7–15)</div>

The lover is not deterred: So taken is he by his rose that he exclaims,
"Might I again experience that bliss and be where I then thought I
was, I vow that willingly I would give my life" (10.139–141). Thus,
the courtly love theme of love as sickness and pain is drawn together
with the feudal imagery: the hero of the courtly love tradition is a
hero of love, willing to endure all for the sake of his Lady.

One of the most characteristic and original features of the courtly love tradition is that love is seen as the source of all virtues and prowess. Love ennobles and empowers. One in love can and will do anything. In earlier literature, sexual attraction was seen as a danger to military prowess. For the courtly love tradition, love for the Lady endues the hero with courage and strength. As Arnaut says, "Each day I am a better man and purer/for I serve the noblest lady in the world."[37] The same notion is expressed in a brief lyric allegedly written by Edward III of England for his son, the Black Prince:

> Love ladies and maidens
> And serve and honor them
> In thought, word, and deed...
> From ladies come prowess,
> Honors and dignities...
> For we hardly ever see a valiant man
> Who does not or has not loved.

Campellanus expands the same notion:

> Now it is the effect of love that a true lover cannot be degraded with any avarice. Love causes a rough and uncouth man to be distinguished for his handsomeness; it can endow a man even of the humblest birth with nobility of character; it blesses the proud with humility; and the man in love becomes accustomed to performing many services gracefully for everyone. O what a wonderful thing is love, which makes a man shine with so many virtues and teaches everyone, no matter who he is, so many good traits of character![38]

As Chrétien de Troyes put it, "All good things come from love."[39]

---

[37] Note the striking claim that an *adulterous* love purifies!
[38] Quoted in Luria, *A Reader's Guide to the Roman de la Rose*, 178.
[39] Quoted in Mott, *System of Courtly Love*, 24.

Conclusion

I began this chapter with a summary of part of Book 1 of the *Faerie Queene* of Edmund Spenser, who is among the greatest English heirs of the romance tradition. Protestant that he was, however, Spenser was unhappy with the unconsummated and adulterous love of the medieval romances, and he pushed romance in an "epithalamion" direction. That is, instead of pitting married love against romantic love, as the courtly love tradition did, Spenser seeks to bring romantic love and passion into marriage. The romantic tales of the *Faerie Queene* do not end tragically with the deaths of the lovers, but with marriages. Spenser's romances are comedies, and in their way, divine comedies.

Dante too "transcends" the courtly love tradition, and he too reshapes the romance into comedy. His method for doing so, however, is quite different from Spenser's, as we shall see.

Review Questions

1. Where and when did courtly love poetry first arise?

2. Did courtly love poetry come directly from Christian influence? Why or why not?

3. What are the main features of the courtly love tradition?

4. Tell the story of Tristan and Isolde.

5. What is meant by saying that courtly love poetry is a "feudalization" of love?

6. What is the story of the *Romance of the Rose*?

CHAPTER 2

POLITICS, PROPHECY, AND THE POETRY OF LOVE

The *Divine Comedy* tells the story of a pilgrimage through the world of the dead. Dante himself is the lead character, and he is guided through Hell, Purgatory, and Heaven,[1] until he reaches the vision of God. Along the way he meets many historical, mythical, and contemporary characters and has the opportunity to comment on their lives and to consider the lessons that can be learned from them. Though the *Comedy* can be fairly easily summarized, it is a highly complex work. Not only does it contain hundreds of characters and incidents, many of them obscure to a modern reader, but it has always been read as a work with several layers of meaning. Many scholars now doubt that the famous "Letter to Can Grande"[2] was actually from Dante's own hand, but if it is not, it represents an early reading of the *Comedy*. The author, supposedly Dante himself, is analyzing the *Divine Comedy* in terms of medieval methods of biblical interpretation. "The sense of this work," he explains, "is not simple, but on the contrary it may be called polysemous, that is to say, 'of more senses than one.'" As he goes on to explain this point, he refers to the common method of medieval biblical interpretation. Israel's escape from Egypt at the exodus, for example, has a fourfold sense: if we inspect the letter

[1] Throughout this book Hell, Purgatory, and Heaven or Paradise refer to the regions of the world of the dead, while the Italian titles *Inferno*, *Purgatorio*, and *Paradiso* refer to the three sections of Dante's poem.

[2] During his exile from Florence, Dante spent several years in Verona, in the court of Can Grande, the prince.

alone the departure of the children of Israel from Egypt in the time
of Moses is presented to us; if the allegory, our redemption wrought
by Christ; if the moral sense, the conversion of the soul from the
grief and misery of sin to the state of grace is presented to us; if the
anagogical, the departure of the holy soul from the slavery of this
corruption to the liberty of eternal glory is presented to us.

Reducing the fourfold to a twofold sense—literal and allegorical, the author explains how the *Comedy* is to be understood:

> [W]e see clearly that the subject round which the various senses
> play must be twofold. And we must therefore consider the sub-
> ject of this work as literally understood, and then its subject
> as allegorically intended. The subject of the whole work, then,
> taken in a literal sense is "the state of souls after death," without
> qualification, for the whole progress of the work hinges on it and
> about it. Whereas if the work is taken allegorically the subject is
> "man, as by good or ill desserts, in the exercise of freedom of his
> choice, he becomes liable to rewarding or punishing justice."[3]

If the letter was written by Dante, there can be no doubting his
self-confidence, for he is claiming that his own poetry manifests
the same richness and complexity as Scripture itself.

Whoever the author was, the "Letter to Can Grande" highlights
something that is apparent to every reader of the *Comedy*—namely,
that there is usually more than one thing going on. Though the
letter uses different terms, it will be helpful to examine the overall
themes of the *Comedy* from three angles: first, the poem is intended
as prophecy of a moral and political kind; second, it reflects Dante's
personal development as a poet and his distinctive experience as a
lover; and third, the poem describes an intellectual and spiritual
development that is to be modeled by the reader.

---

[3] A selection from the "Letter to Can Grande" may be found at the Geoffrey Chaucer
page, www.courses.harvard.edu/~chaucer/special/authors/dante/cangrand.html.

Political Prophecy

Few definite facts are known about the life of Dante Alighieri (1265–1321).[4] This is a curious conclusion concerning a poet who was constantly writing about himself. Nonetheless, though he is the main character in many of his own works, he reveals little that can be taken as historical fact. The *Vita Nuova (New Life)* is an autobiography of sorts, but that work focuses more on his emotional life than on events. Even with regard to his emotional life, it is not always clear how much Dante is expressing his own feelings and how much he is following or satirizing the conventions of the love poetry of his time. Dante is also the protagonist of the *Comedy*, but the Dante of the poem is a literary persona and not identical to the real life human being. Dante is not simply an epic poet in the tradition of Homer and Virgil; Dante is also an epic *hero*. In the ancient world, epic heroes looked forward to the time when bards would sing their praises; with Dante, the hero has become the bard, and he sings a song of himself.

Still, we do know something about the real man. We know that he was a "Renaissance man" in the fullest sense, working not only as a poet, but also as a soldier, philosopher, theologian, lawyer, politician, courtier, and diplomat. His formation as a poet came not only from reading books but from immersion in life. In particular, his political setting and experiences are an important part of the background to the poem.

Dante was born in early Renaissance Florence. His family tree included Cacciaguida, who was knighted during the Second Crusade, but by the time Dante was born the family was neither important nor wealthy. Little is known about his schooling, though he was apparently trained in rhetoric by Brunetto Latini, who appears in *Inferno*, and also read the poetry of the French troubadours and their Italian imitators. In addition, he embarked at some point on an extensive program of self-training, reading widely in theology, philosophy, and history, as well as poetry. As a young man,

---

[4] Much of the information in the following paragraphs is from Mark Musa's "Introduction" to *The Portable Dante* (New York: Penguin, 1995), ix–xvi.

he formed friendships with other poets and artists in Florence, the most important of whom was Guido Calvalcanti.

Both of Dante's parents died before he was twenty, his mother between 1270 and 1273 and his father in 1283, leaving Dante the head of the family. Two years after his father died, Dante married Gemma Donati and had four children—three boys, Giovanni, Jacopo, and Pietro, and one girl, Antonia. According to Mark Musa, "The marriage had been arranged by Dante's father in 1277, well before his death," and Musa goes on to point out that the marriage had little apparent effect on Dante's work: "nowhere in his works does he make direct reference to his wife."[5]

In Dante's time, Florence was a large and prosperous city of some 90,000 residents, a center of banking, and also home to many artists, scholars, and poets of distinction.[6] More importantly, it was a city split apart by political factions. According to Max Weber, the Italian cities of the Renaissance followed the ancient social patterns of Greek and Roman cities. In the ancient city, power flowed along the lines of family descent; blood ties were the basis of political alliance. In many ancient cities, only those who could trace their ancestry to the founding families of the cities could be citizens at all. In Northern Europe, this clan-based civic pattern was overcome in the early modern period as Northern cities came to be governed by guilds of artisans rather than by families. Italian

[5] Ibid., x.
[6] Historian Denys Hays writes: "What made Florence different from Pisa, Lucca, Siena and other Tuscan republics, as well as from Genoa and Venice, was her great wealth and her industrial development. The combination of banking with the manufacture and processing of cloth, especially woolens, had made a large number of Florentines rich, and had turned an ever larger number into proletarians [i.e., poor city-dwellers]. . . . The Florentine banker ventured his money all over Christendom where he also traded; the economy of the city turned on the economy of Europe. Alert, canny, immensely literate in the language of trade, the Florentine merchant was also suspicious in public affairs; the ruling group devised machinery which was designed to avoid the possession of power by a few clans, let alone an individual. Short-term magistracies, a mixture of lot and ballot, meant a perpetual public interest in politics, a perpetual concern for the preservation of what Florentines called 'liberty,' and, of course, a perpetual state of factions, intrigue and uncertainty" (*The Italian Renaissance in its Historical Background* [Cambridge: Cambridge University Press, 1961], 89).

cities, however, never completely overcame the ancient pattern, so that powerful families and alliances of powerful families ruled the city. The result was often blood in the streets, as Montagues fenced to the death with Capulets.

Florence is a leading example of Weber's characterization of early modern Italy. Marguerite Chiarenza has explained the dynamics of Florentine politics:

> Violence would typically escalate in the following way: originally, because of an insult or an act of aggression, two families would become sworn enemies; next, other families would side with one or the other enemy, forming factions; then, these factions would vie for political power within the city and fortify themselves through alliance with one or more factions in nearby cities; finally, more powerful figures, the pope or the emperor . . . . would be called in to support one or another faction.[7]

During the mid-thirteenth century, Florence was plagued by rivalries between groups called the Guelfs and the Ghibellines. In part, this division had to do with different political ideals: The Guelfs were a papal faction, supporting the political claims of the Pope, while the Ghibellines were supporters of the Holy Roman Emperor. But the division had as much to do with wealth and family as with political principles. The Guelf party was made up of minor nobles, merchants, and artisans, while the Ghibellines came from the old nobility of the feudal period. Musa summarizes the struggles of the thirteenth century:

> Between 1215 and 1278 the Guelfs and Ghibellines of Florence had engaged in a bitter struggle for power, with numerous reversals of fortune for both sides, countless plots and conspiracies, and frequent expulsion orders issued against whoever was on the losing side. The Guelfs finally prevailed [when Dante

[7] Marguerite Mills Chiarenza, *The Divine Comedy: Tracing God's Art* (Twayne's Masterwork Studies; Boston: Twayne, 1989), 2.

was two]. Around 1300, however, there occurred a split in the Guelf party into two very hostile factions: the Blacks and the Whites. The Blacks, staunch Guelfs, remained in control of the commune. The Whites eventually associated themselves with the Ghibellines.[8]

From his entry into politics, Dante was a Guelf. At the Battle of Campaldino, the battle that led to the expulsion of the Ghibell-ines, he fought on the Guelf side. When the Guelfs split, Dante sided with the Whites and eventually formed friendships with Ghibelline families. Throughout this period, Dante held a number of posts in the city government. Violent clashes between Guelf factions eventually became so severe that the government exiled leaders of both White and Black groups. Not long after, a new government recalled the exiled White leaders back to Florence. Pope Boniface VII, who had hoped to bring Florence and other cities under papal control, saw the return of the Whites as a threat to his power in Florence, and the pope called on Charles of Valois, brother to King Philip of France, to intervene. While Charles was on his way to subdue Florence to papal rule, the Florentine government sent an embassy to the papal court to ask him to recall the French troops from Italy. Dante was one of the ambassadors, and while he was gone, the Black leaders, with the help of the pope and Charles, regained control of the city. On March 10, 1302, Dante Alighieri was sentenced to death in his absence, and he remained in exile for the final two decades of his life.

For a time, Dante flirted with hopes for a White counter- revolution that would take the city back and allow him to return. He soon became disillusioned with the violence and intrigue of the exiled Whites and abandoned the project. Around 1310, Henry VII, soon to be Holy Roman Emperor, entered Italy and tried to restore order and to impose imperial rule. Dante, as Musa says, "welcomed Henry as a savior," but Henry's expedition floundered and he died in 1313 without being able to take Florence. With Henry's death,

[8] Musa, *Portable Dante*, xiii.

Dante's hopes of a return home also died, and he resigned himself to the status of a permanent exile.

This political background makes its appearance in the *Divine Comedy* in a number of ways. Hell is full of Florentines, and Florence becomes something of a model of the hellish society, characterized by an idolatrous devotion to money and by interminable strife and violence. In canto 26 of the *Inferno*, Dante "celebrates" the greatness of his homeland with bitter irony, urging Florence to rejoice in her worldwide reputation:

> Be joyful, Florence, since you are so great
>> that your outstretched wings beat over land and sea,
>> and your name is spread throughout the realm of Hell!
> I am ashamed to find among the thieves
>> five of your most eminent citizens,
>> a fact which does you very little honor.
>> (*Inferno* 26.1–6)

Florence has achieved a worldwide reputation—for fraud!

The specific events of the Black coup are recorded in canto 6 of *Inferno*, where Ciacco, a Florentine, predicts that the Black Guelfs (called *selvaggio* here, which means "woodland" or even "savage") will drive out the Whites: "After much contention/ they will come to bloodshed; the rustic party/ will drive the other out by brutal means" (*Inferno* 6.64–66). Though the events occurred before the *Comedy* was written, Dante is writing as if his journey through the world of the dead took place in 1300, before the 1302 coup. Dante was specifically charged with "barratry," the corrupt practice of selling civil offices, and barratry is treated at great and savage length in *Inferno*, cantos 21–22.

Dante's political experience left him disillusioned with the idea that the city could function as a unit of political life without direction from a higher authority. Sometime between 1304 and 1307, while in exile, Dante wrote the *Convivio* or *Banquet*. A philosophical work, it was intended as a comprehensive summary of the truths of philosophy, which included Trivium, Quadrivium, science, and theology.[9] Written in a scholastic vein, it was an attempt, like the scholastic theologies of the medieval world, to reconcile all knowledge in one system. The book includes references to Cicero, Boethius, and Virgil, but it is left unfinished, as if reading Virgil inspired Dante to break off his devotion to the Lady Philosophy and to instead attempt to work out his philosophical questions in poetry.

In this treatise, Dante approves Aristotle's view that men are "companionable animals" who attain their end of happiness only in friendship with others. But the need for companionship does not end with an individual looking for a friend. Families, neighborhoods, and cities need to fellowship with other families, neighborhoods, and cities. To achieve this friendship among groups, a single, worldwide monarchy is necessary. Because he already would rule everything, this universal king would be free from covetousness and envy for other kingdoms, and he would work to keep kings confined within the borders of their kingdoms, so that peace should reign between them, and townships should rest in peace, and while they so rest neighborhoods should love each other. And in this mutual love families should satisfy all their wants, and when these are satisfied, a man should live happily, which is the end for which he was born.

Dante called this universal office *imperium*, or empire, and defines it as "the command of all other offices of command." The man who occupies this office would be the "Emperor" (*Convivio* IV.iv).[10]

Dante is not satisfied with this general defense of empire. He wants to restore the *Roman* empire. The Romans, it could be argued, are unfit for this office, since they acquired their empire by force. Dante counters by arguing that the choice for the office of emperor cannot be left to men, but must directly come from the will of God. And, he goes on, it is evident that God has chosen the

[9] The practice of setting a philosophical discussion at a meal or a drinking party goes back to the various *Symposia* of ancient philosophy.

[10] Quotations are from the translation of William Walrond Jackson (Oxford: Clarendon, 1909).

Roman people for this position:

> because no nature ever was or will be gentler in bearing rule, or stronger in upholding, or keener in acquiring it than that of the Latin race (as may be perceived by experience), and most of all that of the sacred people which had an admixture of the lofty blood of Troy, this people was chosen by God for this office. (IV.iv)

As if quoting Scripture, Dante even cites the *Aeneid*, where Virgil records Jupiter's grant of an "empire without end" to the Romans. "Divine Providence," not force, established Rome, and Providence is "higher than all reason" (*Convivio* IV.iv).

Dante's idealization of Rome and the hope for a new emperor are expressed in several places in the *Comedy*. In *Inferno*, canto 1, Dante is trying to ascend a hill toward the sun, but he finds his way blocked by three beasts: a leopard, a lion, and a gaunt she-wolf. It is especially the last that makes him turn back (*Inferno* 1.52–54). Virgil, who is accompanying him, comforts Dante by promising deliverance from the she-wolf:

> She mates with many creatures, and will go on
>   mating with more until the greyhound comes
>   and tracks her down to make her die in anguish.
> He will not feed on either land or money:
>   his wisdom, love, and virtue shall sustain him;
>   he will be born between Feltro and Feltro.
> He comes to save that fallen Italy
>   for which the maid Camilla gave her life
>   and Turnus, Nisus, Euryalus died of wounds.
> And he will hunt for her through every city
>   until he drives her back to Hell once more,
>   whence Envy first unleashed her on mankind.
>   (*Inferno* 1.100–111)

Though the identity of the "Greyhound" (*Veltro* in Italian) is debated, it is clear that he will be the savior of Italy, the Italy that Aeneas fought to conquer. This is not a reference to Christ as deliverer, but to some political savior who will bring an end to the factionalism and conflict of Italy. Some have suggested that Dante specifically has Henry VII in mind.

Even corruption in the church can be corrected by a revived Roman empire. Dante is especially disgusted by the wealth and worldliness of the late medieval popes, and he puts a denunciation and prophecy in the mouth of the apostle Peter, believed to be the first pope:

> He who on earth usurps that place of mine,
>> that place of mine, that place of mine which now
>> stands vacant in the eyes of Christ, God's Son,
> has turned my sepulchre into a sewer
>> of blood and filth, at which the Evil One
>> who fell from here takes great delight down there. . . .
> The bride of Christ was not nourished on blood
>> that came from me, from Linus and from Cletus,
>> only that she be wooed for love of gold . . . .
> Never did we intend for Christendom
>> to be divided, some to take their stand
>> on this side or on that of our successors,
> not that the keys which are consigned to me
>> become the emblem for a battleflag
>> warring against the baptized of the land,
> nor that my head become the seal to stamp
>> those lying privileges bought and sold.
> I burn with rage and shame to think of it!
>> (*Paradiso* 27.22–54)

Peter assures Dante that the ruin of the church at Rome will not last forever. Popes have been wolves in shepherds' garb, but Peter promises that all this will end when "Providence which saved for Rome/ the glory of the world through Scipio's hand,/ will once again, and soon, lend aid, I know" (*Paradiso* 27.61–63). Scipio was the Roman general who defeated Carthage, and in *Convivio*, Dante pointed to this victory as a sign of God's intervention to secure Roman supremacy. Dante hopes for another Scipio, another Roman soldier, to save the church by conquering an enemy more deadly than Carthage.

There is thus a strong moralistic and prophetic dimension to the *Comedy*. Appalled at the chaos of politics, and of Florentine politics especially, Dante condemns the sins and habits that pervert the city and, like a new Virgil, expresses hope for a new imperial order, giving birth to a new *Pax Romana*.

Review Questions

1. How does the author of the "Letter to Can Grande" interpret the *Comedy*?

2. Give a brief overview of Dante's life.

3. What was the political situation in Florence in Dante's time?

4. How does Dante's political experience in Florence influence the *Comedy*?

5. What is Dante's argument for *imperium*?

6. What is Dante's argument for a *Roman* empire?

7. Give an example of Dante's advocacy of a revived Roman empire from the *Comedy*.

She Who Makes Blessed

The *Comedy* has a definite political aspect to it, but it is not a treatise of political theory or simply a poem of political prophecy. It is also, and indeed above all, a love poem, written out of the courtly love tradition that we examined in the previous chapter. Dante is an indirect heir to that tradition, as he acknowledges in the *Vita Nuova* (*VN*). There he mentions his debt to earlier "love poets writing in the vernacular," that is, in the native language of the people rather than in Latin or Greek:

> The first poet to begin writing in the vernacular was moved to do so by a desire to make his words understandable to ladies who found Latin verses difficult to comprehend. And this is an argument against those who compose in the vernacular on a subject

other than love, since composition in the vernacular was from the beginning intended for treating of love. (*VN*, 25)[11]

The fact that Dante wrote the *Comedy* in Italian rather than Latin is a sign that he considered it preeminently a poem of love. Using the vernacular is also a sign that the *Comedy*, though it has an epic scale, is not exactly an epic poem. Epic poetry generally adopts an "exalted style," and Dante was familiar with this convention from his study of Virgil, but he does not maintain an epic tone. Not only does he refrain from using Latin, but there are also clear departures from the high seriousness expected of epic, such as in the slapstick humor of *Inferno* 21–22.

Though the French troubadours were the first to write vernacular love poetry, Dante was drawing more directly on an Italian tradition. Courtly love poetry spread from France to Palermo, and it became the inspiration for the "Sicilian School" of Italian poets. One of the representatives of the Sicilian school, Giacomo da Lentini, captured one of the key themes of Italian love poetry in a sonnet entitled "Io m'aggio posto" ("I have proposed"). That poem affirms the poet's desire to serve God, so that he can enjoy the "pleasure, play, and laughter" of Paradise. At the same time, he has a conflicting desire to be with his lady: "Without my lady I do not wish to go, the one who has a blond head and a clear face, since without her I could not take pleasure," even in Paradise. Conflict between the desire for God and the desire for his lady is resolved in the sestina (the final six lines of an Italian sonnet) when the poet confesses it would be a sin to refuse Paradise but hopes to have the best of both loves: "it would keep me in great consolation, to see my lady be in glory."[12]

From Sicily, the lyric style moved to Tuscany, giving rise to a Tuscan school. Among the Tuscans, Guittone d'Arezzo was a prominent member, and he anticipates Dante in several respects.

---

[11] I am using the translation of Mark Musa in *The Portable Dante*.

[12] The poem is quoted in full and analyzed in Teodolinda Barolini, "Dante and the Lyric Past," in Rachel Jacoff, ed., *The Cambridge Companion to Dante* (Cambridge: Cambridge University Press, 1993), 14–16.

Guittone had first-hand exposure to the Provencal troubadours, not just to the Sicilian imitators. Like Dante, he used his poetry for political purposes, and because of a religious conversion, he moved from love poetry to religious themes. In one poem, he explicitly contradicts the troubadour view that only the lover can be a poet: "I have heard it said by a man considered wise that a man not pierced by Love does not know how to write poetry and is worth nothing." On the contrary, Guittone says, "he who wants to sing well and be worthy should place Justice in his ship as pilot. Put honored Wisdom at the helm, and make God his star and place his hope in true Praise."[13]

Guittone's themes anticipate Dante's, but Dante was a member of a still later movement that goes under the name *stil novo* ("new style"), and its poets by the name *stilnovisti* ("new stylists"). With respect to poetic technique, the *stilnovisti* deliberately rejected the ornate style of Guittone, and in these poets the troubadour interest in carnal love returns. Unlike Guittone, they do not abandon love poetry for theology and religious poetry, but write theologically colored love poetry. Instead of pulling the poet away from God, the lady, they believe, can become a guide toward God and a means of salvation. One of the poems of Guido Guinizzelli, the founder of the *stil novo*, portrays the poet standing before God, defending the exaggerated praise he has given to his lady: "She had the semblance of an angel that was of your kingdom; it was not fault in me, if I placed love in her."[14] This comes very close to blaming God for the poet's idolatry.

In this way, Guinizelli simply removed the problem that da Lentini and Guittone struggled with: "he begins the process of making the lady more like God so that the two poles of the dilemma are conflated, with the result that the lover does not need to choose between them." Having become a sign of God's glory and presence, the lady can be praised in the most extravagant manner, without danger of drawing the poet from love for God. The lady has become

[13] Quoted in ibid., 17–18.
[14] Quoted in ibid., 20.

a "sacrament" of God's presence.[15] These Italian poets have taken a simile ("the lady is like an angel") as the cold, hard truth: The lady *is* an angel.

This is the tradition to which Dante belongs, and his whole poetic career is an effort to write poetry worthy of his beloved. The object of Dante's love was Bice Portinari, known in Dante's writings as "Beatrice." Dante first saw her around 1274, and from what we can tell in Dante's writings, their relationship was quite superficial. He fell desperately in love with her as a boy, but he admired her from a distance, idealizing her in much the same way as the troubadour poets would have done. His love for her was never consummated, for she married another Florentine and later died in 1290, at the age of twenty four.

The *Vita Nuova* is a record of this relationship. The work is a collection of sonnets and *canzone*, which are lyric poems in stanzas with no refrain, written with hendecasyllabic, eleven- syllable lines. Though written over a number of years, the poems were collected together by Dante in a single work. Framing the poetry is a prose commentary that describes his love for Beatrice, recounts the settings of the poems, and analyzes their structure and meaning. Poetic celebrations of the perfection of a lady are common to medieval poetry, but the prose sets the *Vita* off from earlier poetry collections. Prose encourages us to take the sentiments of the poetry with utter seriousness, rather than as the frivolous play of a poet in love.

Two serious themes emerge from this intertwining of poetry and commentary: The book traces the poet's education in love, and simultaneously his training as a poet. At the beginning, Dante is operating very much in the traditional framework of Italian love poetry. The flavor of the *Vita Nuova* is evident in his description of his first sight of Beatrice, and the effect it has on him:

> Nine times already since my birth the heavens of light had circled back to almost the same point, when there appeared before my eyes the now glorious lady of my mind, who was called Beatrice even by those who did not know what her name was. She had been in this life long enough for the heaven of fixed stars to be

[15] Ibid., 21–22.

able to move a twelfth of a degree to the East in her time; that is, she appeared to me at about the beginning of her ninth year, and I first saw her at the end of my ninth year. She appeared dressed in the most patrician of colors, a subdued and decorous crimson, her robe bound round and adorned in a style suitable to her years. At that very moment, and I speak the truth, the vital spirit, the one that dwells in the most secret chamber of the heart, began to tremble so violently that even the most minute veins of my body were strangely affected; and trembling, it spoke these words: "Behold a God stronger than I, who comes to rule over me" . . . . Let me say that, from that time on, Love governed my soul, which became immediately devoted to him, and he reigned over me with such assurance and lordship, given him by the power of my imagination, that I could only dedicate myself to fulfilling his every pleasure. (*VN*, 2)

For Dante, this brief encounter at the age of nine was the moment when he began to live. Later, after a vision of Beatrice eating his "burning heart," his soul "had become wholly absorbed in thinking about this most gracious lady; and in a short time I became so weak and frail that many of my friends were worried about the way I looked" (*VN*, 4). Dante had received the wound and was vassal completely to the God of Love.

But Dante does not remain at this level of passion. As the book continues, Beatrice grows in stature to become a figure of cosmic significance. Nine years after their first encounter, he sees her again and she greets him "so graciously that at that moment I seemed to experience absolute blessedness." When, in the second *canzone*, he dreams of her death, it affects the whole natural world:

Now captured by my false imaginings
and somehow in a place unknown to me,
I was the witness of unnatural things:
of ladies passing with disheveled hair,
some weeping, others wailing their laments
that pierced the air like arrows tipped in flame.
And then it seemed to me I saw the sun

grow slowly darker, and a star appear,
and sun and star did weep;
birds flying through the air fell dead to earth;
and earth began to quake.
A man appeared, pale, and his voice was weak
as he said to me: "You have not heard the news?
Your lady, once so lovely, now lies dead." (*VN*, 23)

It is as if the death of Beatrice repeats the death of Christ.

Dante's association of Beatrice with Christ appears in other passages as well. In *Vita Nuova* 24, he meditates on the name of another woman, Giovanna Primavera, a friend and frequent companion to Beatrice. As Giovanna passes,

> it seems that Love spoke in my heart and said: "The one in front
> is called Primavera only because of the way she comes today; for
> I inspired the giver of her name to call her Primavera, meaning
> 'she will come first' (*prima verra*) on the day that Beatrice shows
> herself after the dream of her faithful one. And if you will also
> consider her real name, you will see that this too means 'she will
> come first,' since the name Joan (*Giovanna*) comes from the name
> of that John (*Giovanni*) who preceded the true light, saying: I
> am the voice of one calling in the wilderness: Prepare the way of
> the Lord." After this, Love seemed to speak again and say these
> words: "Anyone of subtle discernment would call Beatrice Love,
> because she so greatly resembles me."

This is not mere metaphor, nor is it allegory. An allegory would say that Beatrice "stands for" Christ, but Dante is saying that Beatrice reveals Christ and makes Him present. Peter Hawkins comments that "Dante's glorification of Beatrice in the prose goes beyond the bounds of mere idealization. It asks us to take seriously the suggestion that she was no ordinary woman, that she was the singular incarnation of transcendence, and that she was nothing less than Dante's spiritual salvation itself."[16] The implications were not lost

---

[16]Hawkins, "Approaching the *Vita Nuova*," in Jacoff, ed., *Cambridge Companion*, 36.

on the editor of the 1576 edition of the *Vita*, who deleted the portion of chapter 24 that compared Giovanna to John the Baptist and changed the greeting "*salute*" (which means "salvation") to avoid confusing Beatrice and Christ.[17]

How does a nine-year-old girl in crimson grow into a sacrament of the presence of God? The answer is: not easily, and not all at once. Dante's grasp of the significance of his beloved comes only after he follows some false trails to their unsatisfying end. Though he claims to love Beatrice alone, Dante betrays the fact that he had loved several other women. He rationalizes by insisting that the other women are nothing more than "screens" that help to hide his real affections. By showing attention to other ladies, he will deflect attention from Beatrice and prevent anyone from learning the true object of his love. Yet, he composes a poem of lament when one of the ladies leaves Florence (*VN*, 7), and his behavior with another lady is so scandalous that Beatrice stops greeting him in public (*VN*, 10). After Beatrice's death, Dante takes up with a "gentle lady" and nearly forgets Beatrice altogether. This is hardly the behavior of a man whose heart is wholly under the command of one lady! Only when Beatrice appears to him in a vision does he return wholeheartedly to his love for her. As Hawkins points out, the story of the *Vita Nuova* is not so much Dante's unrivaled love for Beatrice as the story of Beatrice's triumph over all rivals.[18]

Beatrice's triumph transfigured Dante's love into a love for a Beatrice beyond Beatrice, a transcendent Beatrice who embodies all goodness, light, and life. Beatrice's early death provoked a crisis for Dante, a crisis that is central to the structure of the *Vita Nuova*. Dante says little of Beatrice's death when it actually takes place. The longer meditation on the significance of her death occurs in chapter 23, when Dante dreams of her death and composes the second of the three long poems in the *Vita* (the other two are in chapters 19 and 31). Centrally located in the poem (chapter 23 out

[17] Charles Singleton, *An Essay on the Vita Nuova* (Baltimore: Johns Hopkins, 1949), 4.

[18] Hawkins, "Approaching," 37–38.

of 42), this poem is also central thematically. From another angle, this poem forms the climactic moment of the book, for it is the last vision of Beatrice's death that Dante sees (see chapters 3 and 12). This structural emphasis points to the fact that it is Beatrice's death that forces Dante to consider what love means, and especially what it means to continue loving Beatrice when Beatrice is no more. As Dante sees it, his love must be transformed into a love for Beatrice as a sign and sacrament of the presence of God. Petrarch ended his career as a love poet, as many troubadours did, with a renunciation of love. Dante will have none of that. He wants no heaven without Beatrice, but, fortunately for him, that presents no problem. After all, the God whose heaven he longs for is the God whose grace Beatrice represents and communicates. He does not have to choose between Beatrice and heaven, for Beatrice has virtually become heaven.

Dante's poetic technique is developing alongside his love for Beatrice. The *Vita* is dedicated to Guido Cavalcanti, Dante's "first friend" and the poet who most influenced Dante's early poetry. Following Cavalcanti, Dante describes the disorienting effects of love and the overwhelming emotional impact of the beloved's presence. For Cavalcanti, however, the lady merely "*inspires* love," but "cannot answer its longings," and thus is "nothing more than a bewitching illusion." Love must thus seek a true object of love beyond the individual woman, in a "transcendent realm" that is "accessible only to abstract contemplation." This is not Dante's mature view. Although Dante describes the effects of love in terms borrowed from Cavalcanti, he is making a very different point. Far from being detachable from the person Beatrice, she is identified with love itself (*VN*, 24), a virtual incarnation of the cosmic reality of love.[19]

If that is true, then traditional love lyrics are not adequate to express Dante's love for her, and Dante acknowledges that the poetry of the *Vita Nuova* falls short. He concludes, however, with hope and confidence that his love will someday find a more adequate expression:

[19] Ibid., 39.

there came to me a miraculous vision in which I saw things that made me resolve to say no more about this blessed one until I would be capable of writing about her in a nobler way. To achieve this I am striving as hard as I can, and this she truly knows. Accordingly, if it be the pleasure of Him through whom all things live that my life continue for a few more years, I hope to write of her that which has never been written of any other woman. And then may it please the One who is the Lord of graciousness that my soul ascend to behold the glory of its lady, that is, of the blessed Beatrice, who in glory contemplates the countenance of the One "who is through all ages blessed." (*VN*, 42)

Whether or not the work that he hoped to write is the *Comedy*, Beatrice is as crucial to the *Comedy* as to the *Vita Nuova*. She initiates Dante's pilgrimage through the world of the dead and serves as his guide when he reaches Paradise. Near the beginning, Dante is hesitant to follow Virgil, and Virgil reassures him by telling him that he has been sent by Beatrice, who, with the Virgin Mary and St. Lucy, form a kind of feminine trinity (*Inferno* 2.49–120). When Dante reaches the top of Mount Purgatory, he sees a great pageant of figures representing the flow of biblical history. At the center of the procession is a "car," and out of the car jumps Beatrice. She has become the central focus not only of the pilgrim, but also of the center of redemptive and biblical history (*Purgatorio*, cantos 29–30).

Even the structure of the *Comedy* owes something to Beatrice. The poem has an obvious tripartite structure; it is divided into the *Inferno*, *Purgatorio*, and *Paradiso*, and this triple structure is also evident in the number of cantos. Overall, there are one hundred cantos, but if the first canto of *Inferno* is seen as an introduction to the whole poem, then the poem consists of three books of thirty-three cantos. The triple structure has deep significance for Dante, since it represents the Trinity. At the stanza level, threes are also prominent. The *Comedy* is written in three-line stanzas, each line of which has eleven syllables (hendecasyllabic lines). Thus, the total number of syllables in each stanza is thirty-three, which matches the total number of cantos in both *Purgatorio* and *Paradiso*. The microcosm of the stanza thus structurally matches the macrocosmic structure of the whole poem, and both are rooted in Dante's Trinitarian numerology.

Structures involving the number "nine" are equally important to the poem. The introductory canto apart, there are ninety-nine cantos, and each subdivision of the world of the dead has nine main sections. These nines are included as a tribute to Beatrice, who, according to the *Vita Nuova*, was mystically connected to the number nine. Dante first sees Beatrice when both were nine, nine years pass until their next encounter, and when she greets Dante at this second encounter, it is 9:00. Depending on how one reckons time, her death could be dated on the ninth day of the month or in the ninth month, or "in that year of our Christian era. . . . in which the perfect number had been completed nine times in that century in which she had been placed in this world." In other words, she died in 1290, when the century had reached the perfect number, ten, nine times. Each of the three visions of Beatrice's death are also associated in some way with the number nine.[20]

After her death, Dante digresses to ask why Beatrice should be so consistently linked with this number:

> One reason why this number was in such harmony with her might be this: since, according to Ptolemy and according to Christian truth, there are nine heavens that move, and since, according to widespread astrological opinion, these heavens affect the earth below according to the relations they have to one another, this number was in harmony with her to make it understood that at her birth all nine of the moving heavens were in perfect relationship to one another. But this is just one reason. If anyone thinks more subtly and according to infallible truth, it will be clear that this number was she herself—that is, by analogy. What I mean to say is this: the number three is the root of nine for, without any other number, multiplied by itself, it gives nine: it is quite clear that three times three is nine. Therefore, if three is the sole factor

[20] Singleton, *Essay*, 14.

of nine, and the sole factor of miracles is three, that is, Father, Son, and Holy Spirit, who are Three in One, then this lady was accompanied by the number nine so that it might be understood that she was a nine, or a miracle, whose root, namely that of the miracle, is the miraculous Trinity itself. Perhaps someone more subtle than I could find a still more subtle explanation, but this is the one which I see and which pleases me most. (*VN*, 29)

All this seems to verge on idolatry, and even verge to the far side of idolatry, but Dante surely did not understand his love for Beatrice as a substitute for his love for God. As he saw it, his love for the human woman raised him up to genuine love for the Creator of the human woman. For Dante, as we shall see, at the heart of the Trinity is the Incarnate Son, the human image of God brought into the life of God Himself. For Dante, this image of God is most wonderfully manifest in his beloved Beatrice, the one whose name means "she who makes blessed."

Review Questions

1. Why does Dante write in the vernacular?

2. Trace the spread of courtly love poetry from France to Italy.

3. How does the love poetry of the *stil novo* differ from early Italian love poetry?

4. Who is Beatrice? What is Dante's relationship with her?

5. Give an example of Dante's use of courtly love conventions in the *Vita Nuova*.

6. How is Beatrice compared to Christ?

7. Why is Beatrice's death important for Dante's development as a lover and a poet?

8. Where does Beatrice appear in the *Comedy*?

9. Explain structures of threes and nines in the *Comedy*.

Out of the Dark Wood

The *Comedy* is, in addition to being a political tract and romantic quest, an intellectual and spiritual pilgrimage. A microcosm/

macrocosm structure runs through the whole poem, so that nearly every event is not only a comment on Dante's world but instruction for Dante, and his readers. Dante is not merely supposed to witness the sufferings of others, but instead must be brought to repentance himself (see *Purgatorio* 30, 142–145).

In this sense, the pilgrim Dante in the *Comedy* functions as a kind of "Everyman" whose experience is to be imitated by others who wish to follow the path toward God. For Dante, the goal of the pilgrimage is the vision of the Christian God, but he also believes that pagan writings are an aid. Most obviously, Virgil, the poet of the *Aeneid*, acts as Dante's guide until he reaches the peak of Mount Purgatory. As noted above, Dante saw himself as something of a new Virgil, heralding the coming of a renewed Roman peace and recounting, as Virgil had (*Aeneid*, Book 6), a journey through the world of the dead.

Aristotle is another key influence on Dante's thought. Aristotle's works were recovered in the West during the thirteenth century. Though initially banned, by the middle of the century they had been approved and were being used by theologians, preeminently by Thomas Aquinas. Dante is an heir to this Christian use of Aristotelian philosophy, and the debt does not go unacknowledged. In *Inferno* 4, Dante sees Aristotle among the other philosophers, and he calls him "the Master of the men who know." The point is made more strongly in *Convivio* IV.vi, where Aristotle is identified as the philosopher "most worthy of trust and obedience" since he above all shows how human life is to be lived. As Dante explains, "the master and artificer who shows us this end and devotes himself to it ought to be of all obeyed and trusted." This master is Aristotle. Etienne Gilson compares the role of Aristotle in Dante's thought to that of the emperor in his political thought. Just as the emperor is to be obeyed by all lesser princes, and just as he brings harmony and unity among them, so Aristotle is a monarchical intellect, commanding all lesser philosophers and harmonizing all areas of study. As we examine the structure of Purgatory, we shall see that the Aristotelian virtues of prudence, justice, fortitude, and temperance are of central importance. Like Aristotle, moreover, Dante insists on the social nature of man, believes that the city is the arena where the ethical life is to be lived, and treats virtue as a mean between extremes of excess and defect. The importance of Christian Aristotelian philosophy is evident from the fact that it is Aquinas who sketches the philosophical outlook of the whole poem (*Paradiso* 13).

Another guide than Virgil or Aristotle, however, is needed to take Dante to the *visio Dei*, the goal of his pilgrimage. After Virgil leaves him, Beatrice takes over, but theologians and mystics also have their part to play. Thomas appears in *Paradiso* 11, and, more elaborately, in canto 13, and St. Bernard of Clairvaux is Dante's personal guide into the highest reaches of Heaven. The structure of the *Comedy* symbolizes Dante's understanding of the relation of philosophy and theology. Philosophy is good and right as far as it goes, just as Virgil is a wise and capable guide to the top of Mount Purgatory. After philosophy, we must move on to theology if we hope to see God and know Him. Dante's pilgrimage and thought are thus structured by a kind of "two-story" view of the world, with "supernatural" truths built on top of a ground floor of "natural" truths.

The Bible is also a pervasive influence in Dante, as in medieval culture generally, and is used in several ways. At times, there are direct allusions which help Dante to explain his experience. As he watches the procession that brings Beatrice to meet him, for example, Dante falls asleep. He describes his awakening using a brief epic simile:

> So, I shall tell you only how I woke:
>   a splendor rent the veil of sleep, a voice
>   was calling me: "What are you doing? Rise!"
> When they were led to see that apple tree
>   whose blossoms give the fruit that angels crave,
>   providing an eternal marriage-feast,
> Peter and John and James were overpowered
>   by sleep, and then brought back to consciousness
>   by that same word that broke a deeper sleep;
> they saw their company had been reduced,
>   for Moses and Elijah were not there;
>   they saw their Master's robe changed back again.
>   (*Purgatorio* 32.70–81)

Though the poetic device is classical (there are no epic similes in the Bible), the content is a tapestry of biblical allusions. The main comparison is between Dante's sleep at the approach of Beatrice and the disciples' sleep on the Mount of Transfiguration (Lk. 9:32). This, of course, brings out a parallel between the "revelation" of Beatrice and the unveiling of the glory of Jesus. But Dante begins the simile by suggesting that the disciples were not waiting to see Jesus' glory, but rather to see the "apple tree" that angels crave. Jesus and, of course, Beatrice are, obviously enough, being compared to a fruitful tree, a tree of life that angels long to taste. Reference to an "apple tree" takes us to Song of Songs 2:3 ("Like an apple tree among the trees of the forest, so is my beloved among the young men") and, even more particularly, to Song of Songs 8:5, where the Bridegroom speaks to the bride, "Beneath the apple tree I awakened you; there your mother was in labor with you, there she was in labor and gave you birth." That Dante intends to echo the Song of Songs is indicated by his reference to the "eternal marriage-feast," a feast on the fruits of the apple tree. The disciples on the Mount of Transfiguration were offered a foretaste of this feast but nearly slept through it. Dante, likewise, has a foretaste of the marriage feast in his reunion with Beatrice, but he is in danger of missing the opportunity.

In some instances, biblical allusions make up larger structural supports for the poem. As Dante watches a boatload of souls being shipped to Mount Purgatory, he hears "'In exitu Israel de Aegypto' /they all were singing with a single voice/chanting it verse by verse until the end" (*Purgatorio* 2.46–48). The quotation is the first line of Psalm 113, which describes the passage from Egypt through the Red Sea, and thus links up the voyage to Purgatory with the Exodus. This in turn suggests that the three large areas of the underworld match the regions of Israel's redemption: Inferno = Egypt, Purgatory = wilderness, and Paradiso = promised land. Only after a time of testing and purging in the "wilderness" of Purgatory will these souls enter the land of milk and honey.

Even Dante's rhyme scheme, known as *terza rima*, may owe

something to his understanding of biblical history and typology. The first and last line of each three-line stanza rhyme and the rhyme of the middle line is taken up as the rhyme for the first and third lines of the next stanza, and so on. A single line closes the canto. *Terza rima* may be diagrammed in this way: ABA BCB CDC . . . YZY Z. Few English poets have attempted to use this rhyme scheme, but there are a few examples. Thomas Wyatt employs it in his "Second Satire":

> My mother's maids, when they did sew and spin
> They sang sometimes a song of the field mouse.
> That for because her livelihood was but thin
> Would needs go seek her townish sister's house
> She thought herself endured to much pain:
> The stormy blasts her cave so sore did souse...

And Percy Shelly's "Ode to the West Wind" follows the same rhyme:

> O wild West Wind, thou breath of Autumn's being,
> Thou, from whose unseen presence the leaves dead
> Are driven, like ghosts from an enchanter fleeing,
> Yello, and black, and pale, and hectic red,
> Pestilence-stricken multitudes: O Thou,
> Who chariotest to their dark wintry bed
> The winged seeds, where they lie cold and low,
> Each like a corpse within its grave, until
> Thine azure sister of the Spring shall blow. . .

Shelley's poem is the more successful of the two, but perhaps these examples will be enough to show why English poets rarely attempt *terza rima*.

By its nature, this rhyme scheme moves the poem forward in a kind of cyclical manner, with each stanza simultaneously looking back to the previous stanza and looking forward to the next. Here again, we have a microcosmic reflection of the macrocosm of the poem, as each stanza echoes the "big tercet" of the entire *Comedy.*

And for Dante, who was thoroughly at home with the medieval figural interpretation of Scripture, each event of history has a similar structure, reaching both back toward Adam and forward to Christ. *Terza rima* is the figural interpretation of Scripture and history worked into a rhyme scheme.

Even when the Bible is not alluded to directly, Christian symbolism is evident in the structure of the poem. In *Inferno* 21.112–114, Dante has a conversation with one of the demons, who claims that "yesterday," five hours from that moment, was the 1266th anniversary of the date when the road was shattered by an earthquake. Though only a passing comment, this date helps us to determine exactly when Dante is moving through Hell. The earthquake that broke the road occurred on Good Friday, and since A.D. 34 was the accepted date of the crucifixion, Dante is letting us know that the action of the poem is taking place in A.D. 1300 (1266 + 34). Medieval Christians believed that after Jesus died He went to Hell to release the saints who had been held there until the way to Paradise opened, and this is the explanation for the earthquake and the toppling of the road. This "harrowing of hell," the demon informs Dante, occurred "yesterday." Thus, when Dante speaks to the demon, it is Saturday, holy Saturday. The anniversary is "five hours from now." Since Jesus died at 3:00 P.M., the demon must be speaking to Dante at 10 A.M. on Holy Saturday, A.D. 1300.

From this information, we can work backward to discover when Dante entered Hell. *Inferno* 2.1–4 tells us, "The day was fading and the darkening air /was releasing all the creatures on our earth / from their daily tasks, and I, one man alone, / was making ready to endure the battle."

Night is coming on again when they reach the end of *Inferno* (34.68–69: "soon it will be night. Now is the time / to leave this place, for we have seen it all"). Dante thus begins his descent into Hell as the sun is going down on the evening of Good Friday, makes his way to the eighth circle by 10 A.M. the next morning, and is leaving Hell as evening falls on Holy Saturday. Dante is following in Jesus' footsteps, going into the realm of the dead on Friday and remaining there through the following day. His pilgrimage is a kind of discipleship; he is following Jesus.

When Dante gets to Purgatory, we expect it to be Easter morning, but it is not. The reason is that Dante has traveled through the center of the earth and ended up on the opposite side of the world from where he entered Hell, in a completely different time zone. The time is twelve hours earlier, and so he begins his ascent up Mount Purgatory as the sun rises on Holy Saturday. Just as Hell is associated with crucifixion, so Purgatory is associated with Jesus' three days in the grave. Through his pilgrimage, Dante is crucified with Christ so that he may ultimately rise with Him.

More general borrowing of biblical imagery reinforces the progression of Dante's journey. Overall, his movement is from the "dark wood" of *Inferno* 1 to the light of God at the end of *Paradiso*. Each canticle ends with *stelle*, stars, and in the case of Hell and Purgatory, the sight of the stars gives a foretaste of the goal, the vision of the One who "moves the sun and the other stars." Other imagery reinforces this movement. As Dante proceeds into the pit that is Hell, mobility decreases and mass increases; people move less and are heavier and more solid. Near the top of the pit, the spirits are too ethereal to embrace, but lower down Dante stubs his toe on the head of one of the people being punished and pulls his hair. At the bottom of Hell, all is ice, frozen solid. Sinners become more solid and immobile as the "gravity" of sin increases. Later, when he begins his ascent up Mount Purgatory, Dante is weighed down, but he lightens as he goes, and he is light enough at the top to rise through the Heavens to the realm of God. According to Aquinas, God is pure act, and Dante depicts this poetically by making heaven a place of dance, a place of constant whirling motion. Dante's ascent to Heaven is an ascent to light and to movement and life, because it is an ascent to love.

Review Questions

1. Why does Virgil lead Dante through the first part of his pilgrimage?

2. Explain how Aristotle's philosophy influences the *Comedy*.

3. How is Dante's outlook a "two-story" philosophy?

4. Give an example of how Dante uses the Bible in the *Comedy*.

5. How does the church calendar give structure to Dante's journey? Why is it important?

6. What is *terza rima*? How does it reflect Dante's interest in biblical interpretation?

7. Explain the imagery of light and darkness, and of movement and rest.

CHAPTER 3

NOT YET AENEAS, NOT YET PAUL
Inferno

Contemporary horror films have nothing on Dante. His *Inferno* is full of terrors that even the most jaded filmmaker would hesitate to put on screen . . . if only for a moment. Nightmarish landscapes flowing with streams of boiling blood, deserts of burning sand showered by fire from heaven, pits and rivers of black pitch, excrement, and muck, a lake eternally frozen. Noxious smells and putrid fogs fill the air, and as he descends toward the center of the earth, light is swallowed in utter blackness. And this landscape is teeming with people shrieking in despair and pain, so many that Dante says in amazement, "I wondered/ how death could have undone so great a number" (*Inferno* 3.56–57). The punishments are terrible: Some are upside down in pits, others are enclosed in flames; some have had their heads twisted so that they face backward as they walk, others are tormented by sadistic demons; some are split from chin to belly, their guts and organs hanging between their legs, and others are chased by ferocious dogs that tear off pieces of flesh; some are transformed into serpents again and again, while others are plagued by disease.

Punishments in Hell are often inflicted by other human beings. The place is full of petty squabbles, foolish arguments, fist fights, hair-pulling, head-butting. Near the bottom of the pit of Hell, Dante comes on Ugolino, who plotted with Archbishop Ruggieri to take over the government of Pisa. When the archbishop turned against him, Ugolino was imprisoned in a tower with his sons and grandsons and left to starve. He watched as his children died "one by one." Dante leaves the final act unspoken, but he says enough: "by then gone blind, groped over their dead bodies. / Though they were dead, two days I called their names. / Then hunger proved more powerful than grief" (*Inferno* 32.73–76). When Dante finds the count in Hell, he is frozen together with the archbishop and gnawing on the archbishop's head:

> As a man with hungry teeth tears into bread,
>> the soul with capping head had sunk his teeth
>> into the other's neck, just beneath the skull.
> Tydeus in his fury did not gnaw
>> the head of Menalippus with more relish
>> than this one chewed that head of meat and bones.
>> (*Inferno* 32.127–132)

Before he can speak to Dante, Ugolino "first wiped off his messy lips/ in the hair remaining on the chewed-up skull" (*Inferno* 33.1–3).

A few cantos earlier, Dante had come upon two men fighting with bestial rage. Dante recalls the madness of Juno and other classical characters and concludes that

> But never in Thebes or Troy were madmen seen
>> driven to acts of such ferocity
>> against their victims, animal or human,
> as two shades I saw, white with rage and naked,
>> running, snapping crazily at things in sight,
>> like pigs, directionless, broken from their pen.
> One, landing on Capocchio, sank his teeth
>> into his neck, and started dragging him
>> along, scraping his belly on the rocky ground.
>> (*Inferno* 30.22–30)

By comparison with Dante, Steven King is as tame as A.A. Milne. Though Dante rivals and surpasses modern horror, his vision of the world of the damned is set in an explicitly Christian context. The violence and terror are not gratuitous or titillating. They are

shown because they teach us about *God*. As he approaches the gate
of Hell, Dante reads the famous inscription:

> I am the way to the doleful city,
>> I am the way into eternal grief,
>> I am the way to a forsaken race.
> Justice it was that moved my great Creator;
>> Divine omnipotence created me,
>> and highest wisdom joined with primal love.
> Before me nothing but eternal things
>> were made, and I shall last eternal.
>> Abandon every hope, all you who enter.
>> *(Inferno* 3.1–9)

For all its horror, Hell is a revelation not only of God's justice and His
wisdom. Hell is a creation of the Father's *power*, the Son's *wisdom*,
and the Spirit's *love*.[1]

For modern people, this sounds preposterous. How could love
construct a place where one man eats the brains of another? In this
reaction, modern readers are not alone. Dante asks himself similar
questions many times during his journey through Hell, and he
reacts to the punishments he witnesses with horror and pity. Unlike moderns, however, Dante believed that if Hell made no sense
to him, the flaw must be in him, not in Hell itself, much less in
God. If he cannot yet see justice and love at work, it is because he
has not learned to see properly. He does not begin with a proper
understanding of love; he must undergo an ascent to love, an ascent
that requires renewed vision.

The *Inferno* is the beginning of Dante's training in right understanding of love, of pity, and of the proper pursuit of knowledge.
We will not be able to examine every episode in *Inferno*, but we will
look at several in detail to see how they mark the steps of Dante's
education. Before doing that, however, it will be useful for us to
examine the overall structure of Hell, and of *Inferno*.

[1] Charles Singleton, *Inferno: Commentary* (Princeton: Princeton University Press,
1989), 40.

Descend, That You May Ascend

The *Comedy* has two beginnings. Dante makes an attempt to ascend in canto 1 of *Inferno*, but fails, and so he has to start again in canto 2. As the poem opens, Dante has come to a sudden recognition that "midway through the journey of our life" he finds himself in a "dark wood" and "had wandered off from the straight path" (*Inferno* 1.1–3). The dark wood represents Dante's condition before he passes through Hell and Purgatory on his way to Heaven, and thus it is a spiritual rather than physical "place." It is his "soul" that is lost and needs help (*Inferno* 1.25, 27). It is significant that Dante is lost in a "wood." Augustine wrote in *Confessions* that "it is one thing, from a wooded mountain top, to see the land of peace and quite another to reach it, when one's way is beset by the lion and the dragon."[2] Like Augustine's pilgrimage toward Christ, Dante's is not merely a philosophical journey, one that can be taken without leaving the ivory tower of the library; it is a journey of discipleship in which he will have to go through the valley of the shadow of death. And it is significant that the wood is dark, for that highlights the fact that he is not only lost but too blind to see where to turn. Dante is not the only one who is lost, however; he is in the midway of "our" life, and the plural pronoun shows that Dante represents all sinners who wish to escape the darkness.

Dante cannot recall how he first lost his way in the wood, but he knows that it occurred when he became "sleepy" (*Inferno* 1.11). When he comes to himself and realizes he is lost, it is as if he is awakening from a deep sleep. Spiritual laziness is part of Dante's problem. When he should have been alert to stay on "the path of truth" (*Inferno* 1.12), he instead decided to sit down for a nap. Even more, the reference to sleep shows just how lost he has been. Getting lost is bad enough. Getting lost and not even realizing you are lost is far worse. But the opening lines of *Inferno* are hopeful. At the very least, Dante has begun to realize that he is no longer on the right

[2] Quoted in John Freccero, "Introduction to *Inferno*," in Rachel Jacoff, ed., *The Cambridge Companion to Dante* (Cambridge: Cambridge University Press, 1993), 172.

path, and that is the beginning of his efforts to find his way out of darkness into light.

And there is a light to follow. As he awakens, Dante sees "morning rays of light" covering a hilltop, and he tries to climb the hill to reach it. Moving toward the light is the right decision, since this light is from "the planet / that leads men straight ahead on every road" (*Inferno* 1.17–18). Following biblical and medieval imagery, Dante spoke of God as "the spiritual sun, accessible to the intellect," and claimed that "no object of sense in all the universe is more worthy to be made the symbol of God than the sun" (*Convivio* III.xii; see Mal. 4:2). Right through to the end of the *Comedy*, Dante's journey will be a journey toward light, the uncreated light that lightens all creation.

Dante also compares himself to a swimmer who has just escaped "dangerous waters" (*Inferno* 1.24). And, after a rest, he begins to climb a "barren slope" (*Inferno* 1.29). The Italian in 1.29 is *la piaggia diserta,* which can mean "desert shore."[3] Later, we discover that the waters are not only "dangerous," but deadly. St. Lucy tells Beatrice of Dante's weeping, asking "do you not see what death it is that threatens him / along that river the sea shall never conquer?" (*Inferno* 2.107–108). Behind this swimming image is the biblical story of the Exodus. Dante is following the steps of Israel under the leadership of Moses: Passing through the deadly sea, entering the wilderness, and then beginning to ascend another "Sinai" into the burning cloud. Swimming also suggests baptism, which was often compared to the crossing of the sea in medieval theology (see 1 Cor. 10:1–4). Dante seeks to escape the deathly Egypt of the dark wood and to find his way through the wilderness to the promised land.

Though the light is Dante's proper goal, the pathway he chooses is not the right one. Three wild animals block his climb—a leopard, a lion, and a gaunt she-wolf—and Dante is forced back down the mountainside. Commentators have suggested that these three animals represent the typical sins in different stages of life. The leopard represents the sins of youth, especially lust. When emotions and

---

[3] Singleton, *Inferno: Commentary,* 9.

hormones are racing in the blood, insatiable desires are aroused and the great temptation is to indulge them. The lion represents the sins of manhood, especially pride. When the emotions of youth have cooled and you have achieved something significant, the danger is that you will become boastful of your achievements and find security in them. The wolf, finally, represents the sins of old age, especially avarice. Passions of youth and the achievements of manhood give way in old age to a love of money.[4] Whether or not the animals represent these particular kinds of sins, it is clear that they represent obstacles to Dante's ascent. He is not yet ready to make that pilgrimage. He will have to spend more time in the dark wood, traveling through places that are darker still.

One reason why Dante is unprepared for the ascent is that he lacks a guide. He does not know how to get back to the "path of truth," and he is still too blind and too sleepy to find it on his own. Aid comes in the form of Virgil. Urged by St. Lucy, Beatrice has sent the Roman poet to guide Dante to Paradise. St. Lucy, whose name is related to the Latin *lux* ("light"), was the patron saint of people suffering from eye diseases.[5] No doubt she is helping Dante because he is suffering from bad vision. St. Lucy is able to heal his blindness. With Virgil's aid, Dante is able to begin his pilgrimage, but Virgil does not lead him up the hillside toward the sun. Instead, Virgil leads him to the gate of Hell, where Dante will first descend before he can begin to ascend. Virgil's guidance is much like that of T.S. Eliot, who advised his modern readers, living in the dark world of the twentieth century, not to avoid the darkness. Instead, the way forward is to move from the partial darkness of this world to the utter darkness. In lines that doubtless allude to Dante (among others), Eliot counseled, "let the dark come upon you / which shall be the darkness of God."[6]

[4] See Dorothy L. Sayers, trans., *The Divine Comedy, I: Hell* (London: Penguin, 1949), 75. Mark Musa refers to commentators who align the beasts with different specific sins: The leopard represents avarice, the lion violence, and the wolf incontinence (*Dante's Inferno* [Bloomington: Indiana University Press, 1971], 6–7).

[5] Singleton, *Inferno: Commentary*, 37. There are saints for everything. St. Barbara was the patron saint of explosions!

[6] From "East Coker, III" one of the *Four Quartets*. See Eliot, *The Complete Plays and Poems, 1909–1950* (New York: Harcourt, Brace, and World, 1971), 126.

Why would Virgil be Dante's guide through the underworld? For Dante, all poets are sages, men of wisdom (*Inferno* 4.110), and therefore suitable guides on the journey that begins in the middle of life. Virgil, moreover, had taken Aeneas through the underworld in the *Aeneid* (Book 6), and there are numerous allusions to that epic throughout the early cantos of the *Comedy*. Virgil's competence goes even beyond this. According to *Purgatory* 7.35–36, though Virgil never knew the theological virtues of faith, hope, and love, he had achieved all the natural virtues.[7] Armed with this moral character, Virgil can be a master to Dante, who becomes his disciple. Finally, Virgil tells Dante later that he himself has been to the depths of Hell to bring a traitor up (*Inferno* 9.20–30).

There is a political reason for choosing Virgil as well. Virgil's epic was about the founding of Rome, and Dante is hoping for a restoration of that empire. When Virgil promises the coming of a future "Greyhound," the "Veltro," he says the Greyhound "comes to save that fallen Italy / for which the maid Camilla gave her life/ and Turnus, Nisus, Euryalus died of wounds" (*Inferno* 1.106–108). These are names of characters from the *Aeneid*—two who fought against Aeneas (Camilla and Turnus) and two who gave their lives in Aeneas's service (Nisus and Euryalus). Virgil mentions Camilla and Turnus to show that he is hoping not only for a restoration of Rome but for a rebirth of the whole of Italy. It is also very characteristic of Virgil to be concerned with the victims of Aeneas's triumph. Camilla and Turnus are noble characters in their way, even though they fall before the advancing forces of fate. Virgil depicts them with sympathy, but he also knows that Aeneas's triumph is according to the will of the gods. This balance of sympathy, and even pity, with a recognition of God's justice and sovereignty, is one of the things that Dante has to learn. Having already written an epic that achieves this balance, Virgil can train Dante as a poet of renewed Rome and a resurrected Italy.[8]

---

[7] This is consistent with Dante's view that one can achieve natural virtue without possessing the theological virtues.

[8] See Marguerite Mills Chiarenza, *The Divine Comedy: Tracing God's Art*, Twayne's Masterwork Studies, (Boston: Twayne, 1989), 25–26.

Physically, Hell is a funnel-shaped pit whose bottom end is at the center of the earth. Satan is frozen in ice at the center, and after climbing past him, Dante and Virgil turn upside down and begin climbing. Thus, after passing by Satan, the worst sinner of all, the descent becomes an ascent. The theme of a descent that turns into an ascent comes from Augustine, who urged his readers to "descend in order to ascend." Humility must, for the Christian, precede exaltation. For Dante, it also means that one must first see the horrors of sin and its punishment before one is able to begin purging those sins and ascending toward God.

Dante and Virgil first reach an area that is not part of Hell proper, known as the "vestibule of Hell." He hears souls shrieking in anguish in the midst of a "whirling storm" and sees "a kind of banner / rushing ahead, whirling with aimless speed / as though it would not ever take a stand," followed by "an interminable train/ of souls" (*Inferno* 3.52–55). Doomed to forever chase a banner that is never still, these are "souls who lived a life / but lived it with no blame and with no praise." Heaven, Virgil explains, "cast them out," and even "Hell itself would not receive them, for fear the damned might glory over them" (*Inferno* 3.34–42). Making choices that exercise the will, is, for Dante, the highest expression of human nature, but these souls belong to people who never chose either for or against God. Because they refused even to use their highest faculty, even Hell is too good for them.[9]

Once past the "vestibule," Dante and Virgil travel through nine main circles that form circular cliffs around the circumference of the pit of Hell. In each circle, sinners who are guilty of a particular kind of sin are being punished in a way that is appropriate to their sin. Some circles, particularly circles 8 and 9, are subdivided further, so that each subsection represents a specific form of the sin that is punished in the circle as a whole. Limbo, the first circle, is not a

---

[9] Many of the poems of T.S. Eliot employ imagery from the vestibule of Hell. Eliot saw the modern world as a place where precisely this kind of indecision was apparent everywhere.

place of punishment, and the people who inhabit it were virtuous in life and are prevented from going to Purgatory or Paradise only because they were not Christians. Virgil comes from Limbo to help Dante, and the place is teeming with other poets and philosophers of the classical world: Aeneas, Caesar, Aristotle, Plato, Cicero, and the Arabic philosophers who helped restore Aristotle to Europe, Avicenna and Averroes. Their only pain is the pain of being denied entry to the presence of God.

After Limbo come the circles for the Lustful, the Gluttons, the Greedy, and the Wrathful. Then come the circles of heretics and the

CANTO	LEVEL	SUBLEVEL	SIN	PUNISHMENT
3	Vestibule		refusal to choose	chase a standard
4	Limbo		pagans	without hope
5	2d circle		lust	blown by wind
6	3d circle		gluttony	rain
7	4th circle		hoarding/spendthrift	rolling weights
	5th circle		wrath	stuck in a muddy bog
8–9	5th circle		wrath	
9	CITY OF DIS			
10	6th circle		heresy	burning tombs
11	7th circle		violence	
12		Phegethon	against neighbors	river of blood
13		Pathless wood	against self	turned to trees
14		Burning sand	against God/blasphemy	lie supine/rain of fire
15–16			against nature/Sodom	fruitless running
17			against Art/usury	look at sand
	MALEBOLGIA			
18	8th circle		simple fraud	
		1st bolgia	pimps and seducers	whipped by demon
		2d bolgia	flatterers	immersed in excrement
19		3d bolgia	simoniacs	head down in fiery pits
20		4th bolgia	sorcerers	head twisted around
21–22		5th bolgia	barratry	boiling pitch
23		6th bolgia	hypocrites	gilded cloaks of lead
24–25		7th bolgia	thieves	snake-bitten, turned ash
26–27		8th bolgia	counselors	wrapped in flame
28		9th bolgia	sow discord	split in two
29–30		10th bolgia	falsifiers	disease
31	DESCENT TO "WELL"			
32	9th circle		complex fraud	
		Caina	betray kindred	up to neck in ice
		Antenora	betrayers of country	deeper in ice
33		Ptolomaea	betray guests	
34		Satan	greatest traitors	in Satan's mouth

violent, and finally two circles for those who committed fraud. This
nine-fold outline, and the subdivisions of Hell, are summarized in
the diagram on the previous page.

Though Hell has a nine-fold structure (in keeping with Dante's
fascination with that number), it is also helpful to see Hell in three
sections. The three main sections are marked out by borders that
Virgil is incapable of passing through without help. At a number of
points in these early circles, Virgil and Dante are confronted by the
guardians of the underworld. Charon, who rows people across the
river Acheron, at first refuses to allow Dante, a living man, to get
into his boat: "you, the living soul, you over there/get away from all
these people who are dead" (*Inferno* 3.88–89). But Virgil is ready:
"it is so willed, there where the power is/for what is willed; that's
all you need to know" (*Inferno* 3.95–96), and Charon relents. They
have a similar encounter with Minos in canto 5 as Virgil and Dante
are moving from Limbo to the circle of the lustful. Minos snarls at
Dante and warns him, "be careful how you enter and whom you
trust/it's easy to get in, but don't be fooled" (*Inferno* 5.19–20). But
Virgil is again capable of handling the situation, by repeating his
rebuke to Charon (*Inferno* 5.23–24). Finally, as they enter the fourth
circle, the circle of the greedy, Pluto threatens them by appealing
to Satan—"Pape Satan, pape Satan aleppe"—and Dante cowers.
After reassuring his disciple, Virgil turns savagely on Pluto:

> Be quiet, cursed wolf of Hell:
> feed on the burning bile that rots your guts.
> This journey to the depths does have a reason,
> for it is willed on high, where Michael wrought
> a just revenge for the bold assault on God.
> (*Inferno* 7.8–15)

Pluto falls to the ground as a sail deflates and collapses when the
mast breaks.

All of these encounters build up Dante's confidence in his
guide, but when they get to the gate of the city of Dis (Hades) the

outcome is not so happy. The inhabitants of Dis oppose Dante's entry. Virgil encourages him, but the people of Dis rush inside their walls and shut the door with Virgil outside. Virgil tries to negotiate a passage, but he returns dejected and defeated. As canto 9 opens, the crisis becomes worse. Furies fly out of the city calling for Medusa and begin to attack the poets. In ancient mythology, Furies are hellish beings who incite people to revenge and violence. Their appearance here is appropriate, for Dante and Virgil are about to enter the city where violence is the rule of the day. Faced with this opposition, Virgil can do nothing more than shield the pilgrim's eyes against Medusa, the sight of whom would turn Dante to stone (*Inferno* 9.55–60).

When all seems lost, help arrives in a mysterious form:

> and then, above the filthy swell, approaching,
>> a blast of sound, shot through with fear, exploded,
>>> making both shores of Hell begin to tremble;
> it sounded like one of those violent winds,
>> born from the clash of counter-temperatures,
>>> that tear through forests; raging on unchecked,
> it splits and rips and carries off the branches
>> and proudly whips the dust up in its path
>>> and makes the beasts and shepherds flee its course . . . .
> As frogs before their enemy, the snake,
>> All scatter through the pond and then dive down
>>> until each one is squatting on the bottom,
> so I saw more than a thousand fear-shocked souls
>> in flight, clearing the path of one who came
>>> walking the Styx, his feet dry on the water.
> From time to time with his left hand he fanned
>> his face to push the putrid air away,
>>> and this was all that seemed to weary him.
> I was certain now that he was sent from Heaven.
>> I turned to my guide, but he made a sign
>>> to keep my silence and bow low to this one.
>
>> (*Inferno* 9.64–87)

Opening the gate of the city with the touch of a wand, the heavenly figure rebukes "Heaven's outcasts, despicable souls," turns, and walks back across the river. What is important structurally in this uncanny scene is that, for the first time, Virgil meets a situation he cannot handle. This, along with the fact that they enter the gates of Dis at this point, makes this passage the first structural division of the poem. All this takes place, significantly enough, in the *ninth* canto.

After moving through the sixth and seventh circles, Dante and Virgil come to the edge of a cliff, over which a river of blood plunges thunderously to the pit below. For a second time, Virgil faces a threshold that he cannot cross without aid. This incident, like the incident at the gates of Dis, involves crossing the threshold of a city, in this case the city of "Malebolgia" or "Malebolge." This time, they receive help from a monster, a beast with a stinging tail (*Inferno* 17.1) that pollutes the whole world. It is identified by Dante as "the repulsive spectacle of fraud" (*Inferno* 17.7). Though his end is dangerous, he has the face of a "just man" with "mild benignity." This is the helper, identified as Geryon, that takes the poets into the Malebolge, carrying them on his back.

Like the deliverance at the gate of Dis, this deliverance foreshadows the coming circles. At the edge of Dis, they were confronted by Furies who instigated violence, while at the edge of the cliff that leads to Malebolge, they are aided by Geryon, a monster who represents Fraud. Apparently the monster, though representing Fraud, is somehow an aid to Dante's journey. Malebolge is an inverted city corrupted by fraud, and Dante's exploration of the corrupted city will enable him to grow in his understanding of the heavenly city. They plumb the depths of corruption in order to transcend it, descending in order to ascend.

Thus, we are given the following overall structure to the canticle:

Furies — Dis
Fraud — Geryon

	——————— Cantos 1–8 ———————
Section 1	Limbo
	Four Circles of Hell
	——————— Cantos 9–16 ———————
Section 2	Incident at Dis (canto 9)
	Two Circles
	——————— Cantos 17–34 ———————
Section 3	Geryon (canto 17)
	Two Circles

This threefold structure corresponds to a moral structure that is explicitly outlined by Virgil in canto 11, when the two poets are standing at the edge of the seventh circle. The central question for Dante is how one has used his will, his power of choice. Men can misuse their power of choice in one of three ways. Sinners in the vestibule have not used their will at all, and therefore they are outside Hell. Circles two through five house sinners who did not sin out of ill will but out of incontinence, an inability to control their desires. Though the things they sought in life were good, their desire for this good was too strong. Thus, these circles punish sins of lust, gluttony, greed, and wrath; that is the order from higher to lower. Lust is an excessive desire for carnal love, which is a good thing in itself but should not become an idol. Gluttony is an excessive desire for food and drink. Greed, an excessive love for money, can manifest itself in two ways. A man who hoards money is greedy, but a man who is careless in spending money is also hoping for happiness from material wealth. Finally, wrath is an excessive desire for the good of vengeance and justice. Thus far the circles outside the gates of Dis.

Within the city of Dis, the four remaining circles have to do with "malicious wrong" (*Inferno* 11.22). Someone acts maliciously when he actually desires to do something evil, and there are two forms of malicious acts: force and fraud (*Inferno* 11.24). The sixth circle, the circle of heretics, seems to stand somewhat outside this structure, but it is within the walls of Dis and is associated with sins of violence. Those who do malicious wrong by force are in circle 7, while those who are malicious by fraud are in the lowest two circles.

All sins displease God, but Virgil tells Dante that God is least displeased with sins of incontinence. Therefore, the incontinent have their place outside the city of Dis. The sins that are punished most severely are those that arise from a malicious will. Among sins of malice, sins of fraud are more serious than sins of force. The rationale for organizing the sins of malice in this way is that man alone can act fraudulently and deceptively, while animals can act violently. Fraud is a distinctively human evil, an evil that defaces in a particularly serious way the image of God in man. Further, Dante believes that the most serious sins are those that are most disruptive of social and political order. Following Aristotle, Dante assumes that man is a social being and the city is the highest point of civilization. Thus, sins that affect the city are more serious and more severely punished.

Review Questions

1. Who made Hell? Why is this an important thing for us to notice?

2. Where is Dante when the poem begins? What does this represent?

3. What does he try to do? What happens?

4. Why is Virgil sent to help him?

5. Describe the physical appearance of Hell.

6. What is the vestibule of Hell?

7. Explain the nine-fold structure of Hell.

8. How is *Inferno* divided into three sections?

9. Discuss Virgil's overview of the moral structure of Hell.

Thought Questions

1. How does Virgil first introduce himself? (*Inferno* 1.67). Why is this introduction significant?

2. How did Virgil find out about Dante's difficulties in the dark wood? (*Inferno* 2.52–74). How does this strengthen the parallels between Beatrice and Jesus?

3. Virgil and Dante encounter three figures from classical

mythology: Charon, Minos, and Pluto. What were the functions of these characters in ancient myths?

4. What is Virgil talking about in *Inferno* 4.52–63?

5. Whom does Dante chat with in *Inferno* 4.85–96? What is Dante saying about his stature as a poet?

6. At the end of canto 11, Virgil talks at length about usury (*Inferno* 11.94–115). What is usury? What are Virgil's arguments against it? Are they persuasive?

Lust, Love, and Pity: Canto 5

As Dante moves through these levels, he encounters various persons of the mythical past, of history, and of his own time. Perhaps the most famous encounter in the entire *Comedy* is with Francesca de Rimini in canto 5. She is the first character in *Inferno* who is allowed to tell her story, and she is the only woman to speak from Hell. Her position at the beginning of the poem emphasizes her importance for the whole *Comedy*. Francesca does not name herself directly, but the information given is sufficient to establish her identity. In life, she was daughter of Guido Vecchio de Polenta, lord of Ravenna during the late thirteenth century. Francesca was married to the deformed Gianciotto de Rimini, son of the lord of Rimini. Her marriage was designed not for love but to end a feud between the two families, but Francesca fell in love with her husband's handsome younger brother, Paolo. Her husband found them together and killed both. When Dante meets Francesca, she is bound together with Paolo, whirling eternally in the wind.

The setting within canto 5 is significant. This circle is for those who have reversed the relation of reason and desire. Instead of subjecting desire to reason, which is, for Dante, the proper order of things, reason has become a slave to desire (*Inferno* 5.39). Dante's view of the relation of reason and desire comes from the tradition of both Greek philosophy and Christian theology, but it is not a biblical perspective. Nowhere in Scripture do we find that reason is superior to man's other abilities and faculties. Practically, reason often follows desire: I first *want* that new stereo system, and then I think about ways to get it. In general, reason and desire are not separable. As the wonderful and generous editor of Canon Press, Doug Jones, has said, reason is shot through with desire, and desire with reason. If they are not separable, it makes no sense to talk about one enslaving another.

The shades in the circle of lust are being blown about eternally by a fierce wind, and this provides a good example of how Dante constructs his punishments. At times, the punishments fit the crime in an eye-for-eye sense. What the sinner did comes back on his own head. Caiaphas, who urged Pilate to crucify Jesus, is himself "crucified with three stakes on the ground" (*Inferno* 23.111). Schismatics, those who are responsible for the division of the church, have their bodies ripped open (*Inferno* 28.1–45). In other cases, the punishment is an ironic reversal of the sin. Soothsayers, who have attempted to look into the future apart from God, have their heads twisted around, condemned forever to look *backward*, unable to see "what was ahead of them" (*Inferno* 20.1–15).

In some cases, however, the punishment is not so much a punishment as an exposure of the true nature of the sin; it shows us what sin would look like once stripped of the illusory beauty that makes it attractive. Punishment, in short, is often inherent in the sin itself, not added to it afterwards. In this sense, Dante's God does not inflict punishment; rather, sinners who choose sin and refuse to repent are inflicting punishment on themselves. This is true of the schismatics, for example, for in life they were in fact rending a real body, the body of Christ. Dividing Christ's body should have been as horrifying to them as seeing a person ripped apart. Likewise, the punishment of the ignorant in the vestibule of Hell, forced eternally to pursue without any goal, is a symbol of the directionless lives they lived. Here in the circle of the lustful, sinners are blown about by the wind, a symbol of how, in life, they were driven by changeable passions. This exposure of the true nature of sin is necessary for Dante's eventual ascent. Traveling through Hell, his vision is being perfected; he is learning to see without illusion.

No matter how obvious sin becomes, however, those in Hell are incapable of seeing it, and that is part of the hellishness of Hell. Francesca excuses her adultery with the comment that she lingered in a tempting situation with her brother-in-law, but that, of course, is part of the sin itself, not an excuse. Similarly, in canto 10, Dante encounters Farinata, a Ghibelline leader who led the Ghibellines to victory in 1260. When the Ghibellines wanted to destroy the city, Farinata opposed this plan, and so he saved Florence. He is a Florentine hero, but Dante has put him in the circle of heretics because he was posthumously convicted of Epicurean heresy, the belief that the soul dies with the body. When Farinata recognizes Dante's accent as Tuscan, he "stood out tall, with his chest and brow proclaiming his disdain for all this Hell" (10.34– 36). Farinata is hardly aware that he is even in Hell.

Sinners in Hell are blind to their sin because they are resistant to their punishment. Michael E. Smith, in an unpublished essay on punishment in the *Comedy*, points out that sinners in Purgatory also suffer, and in fact "most of the punishments in Purgatory are of the same kind as the ones in Hell," since "the same fire that roasts the damned purified the penitents." The difference is not the punishment, but the acceptance of punishment by the sinner. If the sinners in Hell were moved to Purgatory, they would still not repent, because for them the pains "are nothing but evil. . . . The goodness of God and his punishments is beyond consideration."[10] They are locked forever in blindness, a darkness darker than the dark wood.

Francesca comes at the end of a list of other lovers. The first of these is Semiramis, who

> was empress over lands of many tongues;
> her vicious tastes had so corrupted her
> she licensed every form of lust with laws
> to cleanse the stain of scandal she had spread (5.54–57).

[10] Michael E. Smith, "Punishment in the *Divine Comedy*" (unpublished, 1994), 50, 58, 66.

According to one account of her life,

> "she ... most shamefully conceived a son, godlessly abandoned
> him, and then covered her private disgrace by a public crime. For
> she prescribed that between parents and children no reverence
> for nature in the conjugal act was to be observed, but that each
> should be free to do as he pleased."[11]

To cover the scandal of her own incest, she encouraged others in
the same crime.

Her example sets the tone for the other sinners in this circle
since it emphasizes that there are public consequences for lust.
Dante sees Cleopatra, whose seduction of Mark Antony doomed
his hopes to be emperor. There is Helen, "the root of evil woe last-
ing long years," and Achilles, whose love for the Trojan princess
Polyxena led to his death. Paris, whose lust for Helen started the
Trojan war, and Tristan, who loved Isolde even though she was married to King Mark, follow. As Dante proceeds through this circle,
he also sees Dido, the lover of Aeneas, who sacrificed public duty
to love. When Francesca appears, she is in "the flock where Dido
is" (*Inferno* 5.85). Francesca's lust, as much as Dido's, had public
consequences, leading as it did to murder and the breakdown of a
family alliance. President Clinton and the majority of American
people may not believe it, but lust is no private sin.

The connection of lust and violence is underscored by the
connections that Dante makes between the scene with Francesca
and the later gruesome interview with Ugolino. Marguerite
Chiarenza points to a number of connections between the two
stories:

> The pilgrim is attracted by the bestial gesture he finds Ugolino
> engaged in, just as he had been by the light and gentle appearance
> of the lovers carried together by the wind. He had asked to hear

---

[11] Quoted in Singleton, *Inferno: Commentary*, 78. This comes from Paulus Orosius,
whom Singleton calls "one of Dante's chief historical sources."

from Francesca her story of love; from Ugolino he asks to hear his story of hate. Francesca, somewhat insincerely, had claimed that to speak of past happy times would cause her pain; Ugolino warns, most convincingly, that recalling the pain will be almost unbearable to him. Like Francesca, Ugolino agrees to speak, not in the name of love as she had done, but in the hope of causing damage to his enemy. Both are bound eternally to the object of their passion. Finally the verbal echoes are strong: "There is no greater pain than to recall" (Francesca, 5.121–122); "Thou wilt have me renew desperate grief" (Ugolino, 33.4–5); "I shall tell as one may that weeps in telling" (Francesca, 5.126); "thou shalt see me speak and weep together" (Ugolino, 33.9); "the fair form that was taken from me, and the manner offends me still" (Francesca, 5.101–2); "how cruel was my death, thou shalt hear and shalt know if he has offended me"(Ugolino, 33.20–21).[12]

A story of lust is more seductive than a story of cannibalism, but the links show us that Dante sees the two stories together. We will not truly understand the nature of Francesca's sin unless we see that there is an inner connection between it and the sins of Ugolino. We will be making progress in truth when we realize that lust devours.

Francesca and Paolo were tempted to adultery by reading the story of Lancelot and Guenevere, and especially a portion of the story concerning Galleot, who served as an intermediary between the two legendary lovers.[13] As Francesca and Paolo read of the "smile" of Guenevere that was kissed by the great lover Lancelot (*Inferno* 5.133), they were led to enact the book in reality. The book thus becomes the "Galleot" of their affair, the "pander" between them, the pimp that enabled their adultery. As we shall see throughout the *Comedy*, imagination plays a key role in making evil look attractive, and chivalric romance or courtly love poetry can be particularly seductive. Learning to see also means learning to judge beauty rightly, to see through a thin veil of beauty to the ugly reality beneath.

---

[12] Chiarenza, *Tracing*, 49.

[13] Boccaccio called the *Decameron* a "Galleot" after this intermediary between Lancelot and Guenevere.

That insight comes later, however, and here near the top of the pit of Hell, it is easy to be seduced by appearances. Francesca speaks, after all, about love, and she speaks movingly and poetically. *Amor* ("love") begins three terzina of her speech, and she declares two laws of love, both of which are themes of courtly love. First, she states the theory that love is irresistible attraction to the beauty of the other sex: "Love, quick to kindle in the gentle heart,/ seized this one for the beauty of my body" (*Inferno* 5.100–101). Francesca is not only alluding to the general tradition of courtly love, but specifically to the poetry of Guido Guinizelli, the founder of the *stil novo*, one of whose canzone affirmed that love takes its residence in "the gentle heart." Her second "law" of love is equally indebted to the courtly love tradition: "Love, that excuses no one loved from loving,/ seized me so strongly with delight in him,/ that, as you see, he never leaves my side" (*Inferno* 5.103–105). A beloved woman is as irresistibly drawn to the lover as the lover is to her beauty. Both laws, it must be noted, attribute omnipotence to love and, at the same time, shift blame from the lovers to the love itself.[14] Following these "laws" of love is disastrous. The final tercet that begins with *amor* speaks of the horrific consequences: "Love led us straight to sudden death together" (*Inferno* 5.106).

Love is clearly a central theme in the *Comedy* from beginning to end. Already in canto 2, Beatrice has sent Virgil to help the pilgrim out of the Dark Wood, and she says that love moved her and made her speak. Beatrice thus has already defined the meaning of love as the divine love that moves Beatrice to rescue the pilgrim. Indeed, Beatrice has gone from her place in Paradise to Hell in order to request Virgil's help (*Inferno* 2.52–54), an act of love that mirrors Christ's own humiliation. Further, the inscription over the gate to Hell indicates that it is a creation of God's love. The *Comedy* ends with an invocation of this same love, the last line of *Paradiso* 33: "by the love that moves the sun and other stars." Dante's journey begins with Beatrice's love, a love that springs from divine

---

[14] Singleton, *Inferno: Commentary*, 89–90.

love, and moves toward the love that moved Beatrice and all other stars. Here in canto 5, however, the love of which Francesca speaks is not that of Beatrice. She insists on the word, but the word has become a cover for carnal lust and ultimately for violence. When she speaks like a romance heroine, we must always remember that Francesca is in Hell. She is winningly hardhearted, but no less hard for that.

Dante has not yet learned to discern between true love and false. As he questions Francesca, he accepts her account of the situation: "tell me, in that time of your sweet sighing / how, and by what signs, did love allow you / to recognize your dubious desires?" (*Inferno* 5.118–120). He "joins her in speaking the language of courtly love. It was love, as she had said, that brought the lovers to 'one death.'"[15]

Nor has he really understood the nature of *pietà*, another key term in this episode, which ranges in meaning from "pity" to "piety." When Dante calls out to Francesca and Paolo, it is with a compassionate cry (*Inferno* 1.87), and Francesca welcomes the *pietà* that the pilgrim expresses for her wretchedness (*Inferno* 1.93). When Dante has heard her story, he weeps with "tristo e pio," sadness and pity (*Inferno* 1.117). "*Pietà*" too is a major theme of the poem. Beatrice's love for Dante expresses itself in pity for his desperate condition in the dark wood. When she finally meets him at the top of Mount Purgatory, she rebukes him with bitter, sharp pity ("pietade acerba," *Purgatorio*, 30.81). The *pietà* of Beatrice ensures that the pilgrim will make his way to salvation, but this is precisely what the *pietà* of Francesca does not do. Instead of rousing him to continue the pilgrimage, Dante ends the canto in a swoon.

Learning true *pietà* takes considerable time. Later, when Dante laments the disfigurement of the human form that he sees in the Soothsayers, whose heads have been turned backwards, Virgil rebukes him:

---

[15] Ibid., 92.

So you are still like all the other fools?
In this place piety lives when pity is dead,
      for who could be more wicked than that man
      who tries to bend the divine will to his own!
                    (*Inferno* 20.27–30)

A more literal translation is that of Charles Singleton: "Here pity lives when it is altogether dead."[16] The only true "piety" is to kill false "pity" for those who are being justly punished and to submit to the justice of God's will.

An association with Aeneas is also in the background. In canto 2, Dante hesitates to enter Hell, telling Virgil, "I am not Aeneas, I am not Paul" (2.32). The reference to Aeneas is an allusion to that hero's journey to the underworld in *Aeneid*, Book 6, and the Pauline reference is to his ascension to the third heaven (2 Corinthians 13). Dante believes he is unqualified to make the journey to Hell and Heaven, his being neither an Aeneas nor a Paul. Though the word *pieta* does not appear here, Dante was well aware that Aeneas's great heroic virtue was his piety (Latin, *pietas*), which was manifested in his willingness to shoulder responsibilities, act out of loyalty to his family and city, and submit to the will of the gods. Piety in this sense is echoing in the background, especially since Francesca is a member of "Dido's flock." Her *pieta*, the *pieta* she rouses, is not loyalty to family and duty or submission to God, but the opposite. Her story of un-*pietas* arouses Dante's *pieta*.

All of this to say that the pilgrim has only just begun his pilgrimage. He has a long way to go before he reaches maturity. He has yet to see sin for what it is. Truly, he is not Aeneas, for he does not know the meaning of *pietas*. Or, he is like the Aeneas of the early books of the *Aeneid*, distracted from his goal and destination by "one of Dido's flock." Nor is he Paul, for he is not yet capable of discriminating true love, true charity, from the carnal *amor* of Francesca.

[16] Singleton's translation of the *Inferno*, with Italian on the facing page, is published by Princeton University Press (1989).

Readers of the *Comedy* have always been attracted to Francesca. Dante meant us to be. But he also meant for us to learn that this attraction is a symptom of our blindness. If we find her attractive, it is because we are still wandering in the dark wood, having lost the path of truth. If we pity her, it is because we have not learned the meaning of true pity; if we think that her love was genuine love, we have not learned the true nature of charity. With Dante, each reader has to confess, "I am not Aeneas; I am not Paul."

Review Questions

1. Who was Francesca de Rimini? What happened to her?
2. Explain the logic behind the punishment of sinners in Hell.
3. Who is with Francesca in the circle of the lustful? What do they have in common?
4. How do Francesca and Paolo become lovers?
5. What is the connection between Francesca and Ugolino?
6. What does Francesca mean by "love"? Is this Dante's view?
7. Explain the significance of the word *pieta*.
8. What does Dante mean when he says, "I am not Aeneas, I am not Paul"?

Thought Questions

1. What does Virgil say about fortune in *Inferno* 7.67–99?
2. Who are the sinners blowing bubbles from under the mud in *Inferno* 7.115–126? What are they doing in the circle of wrath?
3. Farinata is in the circle of heretics, yet much of the discussion has to do with politics. What is the connection? (*Inferno* 10.22–51)
4. Who is Pier Delle Vigne? (*Inferno* 13.31–78) How does his experience parallel Dante's? What should Dante learn from this encounter?
5. Where do the rivers of Hell come from? (*Inferno* 14.94–120).

I Am Not Ulysses

The cantos on the circles of violence describe a horrific natural landscape. The sins of circles 6–7 are bestial. Heresy, especially Epicureanism, is implicitly bestial because it denies man's eternal soul, and this is why it is linked with the circle of violence, which is openly bestial. Once Virgil and Dante ride Geryon down the cliff to Malebolgia, however, they enter a city.[17] Horrible as sins of violence are, Dante is more horrified by the sins of circles 8–9. These are urban sins, and Dante is showing us that while the city tames some of the bestial tendencies of sinful man, it provides opportunities for other types of sin. These latter forms of vice, sins that prey on a society, are, to Dante, the worst of all.

The last half of *Inferno* is devoted to two circles of Hell, the circles of fraud. Fraud is, like violence, subdivided. There are two large categories of fraud and many minor sub-categories. The first of the two main types is called "fraud simple"; it represents fraud or deception of others with whom one has no special bond. This sort of fraud violates the bond of love that all humans are to have with all other humans, but it does not violate any more particular bond. Hypocrites, flatterers, dealers in sorcery, panders (those who aid adulterous lovers to achieve their desires), cheats, simoniacs, and barrators are all included here. Complex fraud violates not only this bond of common humanity, but also is a sin against a special covenant or bond of love. Those who have committed various sorts of fraud are found in ditches that circle the rim of Hell. With one exception, these ditches, called "pockets" or *bolgia,* have bridges over them so Dante and Virgil can observe the sinners from the safety of a bridge above. *Bolgia* is doubly significant, for the word means not only "ditch" but "purse," and therefore the meaning points to the fact that many of the sins punished here are sins involving financial deceit.

Among the important characters in Malebolgia is Ulysses, or Odysseus. Virtuous pagans like Virgil, Homer, and Aristotle are in

---

[17] Robin Kirkpatrick, *Dante: The Divine Comedy* (Cambridge: Cambridge University Press, 1987), 70.

Limbo, but Dante places the heroes of pagan epics lower in Hell. Achilles is in the circle of the lustful, but Odysseus is far down in the depths of the pit. He is, after all, the man of many devices, the trickster hero of Greek legend. The first plot mentioned in canto 26 is his deception of the Trojan horse, a deception that led to the destruction of Troy. This treachery was turned providentially to good, since the defeated Trojans gave birth to Rome, which in turn became the center of Christian civilization. But the Trojan horse episode is not the focus of attention. Instead, Dante tells the story of Ulysses' final voyage, when he persuaded his men to travel beyond the pillars of Hercules into the open sea. His journey ended in death, when Ulysses' ship wrecked on the shores of Mount Purgatory.

Ulysses' story raises some important questions about Dante's own "voyage." The Greek hero encourages his men to "pursue virtue and knowledge" (*Inferno* 26.120), something that Dante himself should approve of. In fact, he begins the *Convivio* by quoting Aristotle's comment that all men desire knowledge, since "everything, being impelled by foresight belonging to its own nature, tends to seek its own perfection. Wherefore inasmuch as knowledge is the final perfection of our soul in which our final happiness consists, all men are naturally subject to a desire for it" (I.i). Only two cantos later, Virgil explains that Dante's voyage through Hell is, like Ulysses' voyage, a way of gaining experience of both virtue and vice (*Inferno* 28.48–50). Not only does Dante encourage the pursuit of knowledge, he describes it elsewhere using sea-faring imagery that reminds us of Ulysses.[18] This is especially evident in *Paradiso*. Dante begins by warning about the dangers of his quest for the highest poetry and the highest knowledge, the knowledge of God:

> All you who in your wish to hear my words
> have followed thus far in your little boat

[18] Peter Dronke, *Dante and Medieval Latin Traditions* (Cambridge: Cambridge University Press, 1986), 20–24.

behind my ship that singing sails these waters,
go back now while you still can see your shores;
   do not attempt the deep: it well could be
   that losing me, you would be lost yourselves.
I set my course for waters never traveled;
   Minerva fills my sails, Apollo steers,
   and all nine Muses point the Bears to me
Those few of you who from your youth have raised
   your eager mouths in search of angels' bread
   on which man feeds here, always hungering,
you may, indeed, allow your boat to sail
   the high seas in the furrow of my wake
   ahead of parted waters that flow back.
                     (*Paradiso* 2.1–15)

He sets out even though, as Aquinas will later tell him, the end of the journey is as yet unknown and the voyage itself is dangerous: "I have seen a ship sail straight and swift / over the sea through all its course, and then, / about to enter in the harbor, sink" (*Paradiso* 13.136–138).

Dante, it seems, is just another Ulysses. If so, what is wrong with Ulysses' voyage? Why is he in Hell, and so low? One key to understanding this comes before Dante ever encounters Ulysses. Dante is lamenting the state of Florence, but he realizes that he cannot let his grief get the better of him. Instead, "more than ever I restrain my talent / lest it run a course that virtue has not set" (*Inferno* 26.21–22). Though not directly a comment on Ulysses, it anticipates him, for unlike Virgil and Virgil's hero Aeneas, Ulysses shows no sense of limits, no *pietas.* After his return to Ithaca, he admits that

not sweetness of a son, nor reverence
   for an aging father, not the debt of love
   I owed to Penelope to make her happy,

could quench deep in myself the burning wish
to know the world and have experience
of all men's vices, of all human worth.
(*Inferno* 26.94–99)

Piety, for Dante and Virgil, is expressed in loyalty to family, but
Ulysses shows no such "reverence." His voyage itself is an exercise in
hubris, in the breaking of limits: Though "Hercules put up his signal
pillars / to warn men not to go beyond that point" (26.108–109),
Ulysses goes beyond them anyway. Unlike Ulysses' voyage, Dante's
is a training in submission to the will of God, a training in piety.
Dante's journey is more like Ulysses' earlier efforts to get home to
Ithaca; for in sailing toward Paradise, Dante is sailing home. His
ascent toward Beatrice is a voyage toward his own Penelope, his
own Ithaca.

Ulysses ends with shipwreck. Intriguingly, Dante began his
pilgrimage by escaping "drowning." As we saw above, escaping
from the dark wood at the beginning of *Inferno*, Dante compares
himself to "a swimmer" (*Inferno* 1.22–24). In the ancient epics,
Ulysses and Aeneas both escape shipwreck by swimming to shore.
They therefore are able to continue their quests. But the Ulysses
in canto 26 ends in the water, incapable of swimming to safety.
His heroic lust for adventure ends where the pilgrimage of faith
begins.

As in the Francesca episode, part of what is going on here is an
account of Dante's own spiritual growth. In the Francesca episode,
he criticizes a brand of romantic poetry that he himself had written.
Here, he criticizes, without rejecting, the quest for knowledge that
he says is a basic human desire. Where Ulysses is at fault is in his
failure to bow to a guide, his tendency to run beyond the limits of
virtue. He has a "burning wish / to know" (*Inferno* 26.97–98). Given
Dante's Augustinian background, this restless itch would have been
seen as a variety of lust; curiosity, Augustine says in the *Confessions*
(Book 10), is a species of lust. Dante may not yet be Aeneas, but
Ulysses' story is a warning that the only safe voyage is a pious voyage. Dante will make sure that he will not end up a Ulysses.

One oddity needs to be cleared up: Ulysses is condemned to Hell for overreaching the limits of knowledge, but he is located in the circle of fraud. In what way does Ulysses commit fraud? The answer is that his speech to his men, urging them to accompany him on his voyage, is a fraudulent speech. This speech begins with a virtual quotation from the speech of Aeneas to his men in *Aeneid*. Dante's Ulysses says, "Brothers, who through a hundred thousand / perils have made your way to reach the West" (*Inferno* 26.113–114), while Aeneas says, "Friends and companions, have we not known hard hours before this?" (*Aeneid* 1.270–271).[19] But this very similarity points out his difference from Aeneas. Aeneas assures his men that they are heading for a destination that the fates have decreed, a new Troy. His adventures are grounded in *pietas*, submission to the will of the gods. As we have seen, Ulysses' voyage is, by his own confession, a rejection of *pietas*. This difference is made all the sharper by the fact that Virgil listens with the pilgrim to Ulysses' speech.

Ulysses' speech offers neither goal nor method, but only inflames his men with keenness for the voyage. This is all he wants to achieve. He claims to be leading his men on a voyage toward virtue, knowledge, and experience, yet he turns his back on the true goal of all voyaging, which is to arrive home, to build a city, or to enter more deeply, as Dante is, into knowledge of God. The pagans who make constructive contributions to human life are in Limbo, but Ulysses is not. His treachery and deception are heightened by repeated uses of the word "little," especially line 122, where he refers to his "little speech" (*orazion picciola*). His "little speech" to his men is really a sign of great *hubris*, refusal to recognize limits of any kind, a rejection of *pietas*. It is a little speech of gargantuan pride, and by filling his men with promises that he cannot keep, he is guilty of fraud against his men.

---

[19] I am using the translation and line numbers from Robert Fitzgerald (New York: Everyman's Library, 1992).

Review Questions

1. What is Malebolgia?
2. What is the difference between simple and complex fraud?
3. Why did Ulysses want to go on another voyage?
4. What was wrong with Ulysses' final journey?
5. How is Ulysses guilty of fraud?

Thought Questions

1. What sin is being punished in canto 19? Who speaks to Dante? Who does he think Dante is? (*Inferno* 19.52–54)
2. How does Virgil help Dante in canto 24.22–27? What does this say about their relationship?
3. What is the punishment for the thieves in canto 25? What does it signify?
4. What is Ulysses' punishment? How is this an appropriate punishment for his sin?
5. Who is with Ulysses? Why?

Into the Well, Cantos 31–34

The final circle of Hell is the circle of those who are guilty of complex fraud. All of them are frozen to varying degrees in the lake or "pool," Cocytus, into which the rivers of Hell empty (see *Inferno* 14.115–120).[20] Cocytus is divided into four concentric circles of ice which hold traitors against family, country, guests, and masters. At the center is Satan, who is stuck at the very center of the earth, with his top half visible from Hell and his legs and feet extending into the southern hemisphere.

As Dante and Virgil enter the "well" (*Inferno* 31.32), Dante sees what he believes to be towers. Again, his sight needs correcting, and as he gets closer he realizes that he has been looking at giants who stand guard around the bank of the well. As he contemplates the size of one giant, he is relieved that Nature has "cast away the

---

[20] The Italian is *stagno*, a word for pond rather than for river or stream.

mold / for shaping beasts like these." They are far more dangerous than giant animals like whales and elephants, for they combine "the faculty of intellect" with "brute force and evil will," a combination that "no man can win against" (*Inferno* 31.49–57). This highlights the reason why the sins of the ninth circle are so utterly evil. Beasts are destructive and violent, but only man combines intellect and evil will with brute force to defraud the ones who are closest to him. As someone once said, the corruption of the best is the worst.

One of the giants attempts to speak, but it comes out like a magic show spell: "*Raphel may amech zabi almi!*" (*Inferno* 31.67). After rebuking the giant, Virgil explains to Dante that "He is Nimrod, through whose infamous device / the world no longer speaks a common language" (*Inferno* 31.77–78). Virgil is referring to the tower of Babel episode (Gen. 11:1–9), and to the founder of Babel, Nimrod (Gen. 10:10). Though he is called a "mighty hunter" in Scripture, there is no indication that Nimrod is a giant. Ironically, though, Dante has mistaken Nimrod for the tower he tried to build. That identity of sinner and sin helps explain why Nimrod is in the ninth circle. He helped build the tower in order to reach to heaven and make a name for himself, but this effort was an assault on the rule of God. Like the giants who are also confined in the well for rebelling against Zeus, Nimrod is guilty of treachery against a heavenly Master, and rightly consigned to the well. Instead of building a tower to Heaven, he stands like a tower among the lowest in Hell.

The result of his sin is equally important for Dante's purposes. Language is the chief means for forming alliances and bonds among men. If we want to make peace with an enemy, we write a treaty; if we want to enter into a marriage covenant, we say "I do" to the spoken vows; if we want to affirm our faith together in the Word, we say "Amen" in unison. Up to the time of Babel, common language bound the nations of the world together. Because of Nimrod's treachery, there is no longer a common language, and it is more difficult for nations to understand one another and to be unified. Few acts of treachery have had such fundamental and permanent effects on the social and political world as Nimrod's. Dante, believing with Aristotle that man is made for community, and believing with Paul that God formed the nations from one man and of one blood, sees the tower of Babel as a frontal assault on the community of man.

Nimrod's assault on mankind is bad, but he is not the lowest of the low. At the very bottom of the pit is Satan, flapping enormous wings that "lock Cocytus eternally in ice" (*Inferno* 34.52). When Dante sees him, he nearly dies: "I did not die—I was not living either" (*Inferno* 34.25). In Paradise, Dante will see unspeakable beauty; here he sees unspeakable ugliness:

> If once he was as fair as now he's foul
>   and dared to raise his brows against his Maker,
>   it is fitting that all grief should spring from him.
> Oh, how amazed I was when I looked up
>   and saw a head—one head wearing three faces!
>   One was in front (and that was a bright red),
> the other two attached themselves to this one
>   just above the middle of each shoulder,
>   and at the crown all three were joined in one:
> The right face was a blend of white and yellow,
>   the left the color of those people's skin
>   who live along the river Nile's descent.
>   (*Inferno* 34.34–45)

Satan, as Dante describes him, does Janus one better, for he has three faces instead of two. He is an infernal imitation of the Trinity.

It is no wonder that Satan is in the circle of the traitors, for he was himself the greatest of traitors. But others are very close to the center. In each of Satan's three mouths he is munching a human traitor. The front face, the red one, is chewing on Judas Iscariot, who betrayed Jesus. Judas is the worst off, since his head is actually inside the mouth of Satan's red face (*Inferno* 34.61–63). In the mouth of the black face Satan is chewing on Brutus, and in the yellow face is Cassius, the other main conspirator against Julius Caesar. If Satan is responsible for plunging the human race into sin, Judas

and the two Roman traitors are responsible for the greatest evils of
human history. Judas conspired to kill his Master, who was Satan's
own Master; Judas was a traitor to the head of the church. Brutus
and Cassius conspired against the first of the Roman emperors, and
thus they attacked God's instrument in the political arena. With
Nimrod, these traitors are responsible for the social and political
evils that plague Dante's world.

What follows is one of the most bizarre scenes in a bizarre poem.
Dante takes hold of Virgil's neck, and Virgil

> he grabbed the shaggy sides of Satan;
> > then downward, tuft by tuft, he made his way
> > between the tangled hair and frozen crust.
> When he had reached the point exactly where
> > the thigh begins, right at the haunch's curve,
> > my guide, with strain and force of every muscle,
> turned his head toward the shaggy shanks of Dis
> > and grabbed the hair as if about to climb—
> > I thought that we were heading back to Hell.
> > (*Inferno* 34.73–81)

Odd though the scene is, it is thematically consistent with everything that has gone before it. Satan becomes the "stairs" (*Inferno*
34.83) by which Dante and Virgil can escape from Hell. Though
Satan is himself evil incarnate, like Hell, he serves a good and useful
purpose in God's plan. This is Dante's version of the theory of the
"fortunate fall," the idea that the fall of Satan and of man turns out
for the best, that it is a "fortunate" thing that man fell. Precisely
because Satan has fallen to the center of the earth, he becomes a
staircase to pass through the center.

Dante is puzzled, however, when he sees Virgil turn and seem to
begin climbing back into Hell: "I raised my eyes, expecting I would
see / the half of Lucifer I saw before. / Instead I saw his two legs
stretching upward" (*Inferno* 34.88–90). Virgil explains to him that
they have passed the center of the earth and are now moving in the
opposite direction. Quite literally, the descent into Hell, the descent
along the shaggy body of Satan, has become an ascent. And not only

an ascent, but an ascent toward sunrise, which is just breaking out over the southern hemisphere as Virgil and Dante emerge (*Inferno* 34.118; *Purgatorio* 1.13–18). Dante is forced to take a roundabout route, but he is heading toward the same "bright world" that he set out for when he first started climbing the hillside to escape from the dark wood:

> We climbed, he first and I behind, until
>   through a small round opening ahead of us
>   I saw the lovely things the heavens hold,
> and we came out to see once more the stars.
> (*Inferno* 34.138)

Review Questions

1. Describe the physical landscape of the ninth circle.

2. What does Dante first think the giants are? Why is this significant?

3. Who is the first giant that Dante and Virgil speak to? What did he do?

4. Describe the appearance of Satan.

5. Who are in the mouths of Satan? Why?

6. What happens when Dante and Virgil climb over Satan? Why is this significant?

7. What is meant by the "fortunate fall"?

Thought Questions

1. What does Dante say about Achilles' lance in *Inferno* 31.1–6? What is he comparing it to?

2. Who helps Dante and Virgil get down into the well? (*Inferno* 31.91–135). Why is this significant?

3. What are the names of the different regions of Cocytus? (see *Inferno* 32.59). What do they mean?

4. Why is Dante surprised to find Friar Alberigo in Hell? (*Inferno* 33.118–138). What is the friar's explanation?

5. What happened to the land when Satan fell into Hell (*Inferno* 34.121–126). How does this fit with the idea of a "fortunate fall"?

CHAPTER 4

REDEEMED FROM FIRE BY FIRE
Purgatorio

Scripture nowhere speaks of Purgatory, and until the mid-twelfth century, Christians did not think of it as a separate part of the world of the dead. Early medieval Christians believed that purging or purification took place after death, but it was thought to be done along the borders of Hell or Heaven and not in a distinct place.[1] By Dante's time, Purgatory had become a distinct location, but for most of Dante's contemporaries, it would have been a temporary form of Hell, a place of punishment and penance prior to one's ascent to Heaven.[2] Not so for Dante. For Dante, Purgatory is not a place of punishment but a place of movement, progress, and sanctification.

Dante's imagery in *Purgatorio* underlines this theme. Neither sun nor stars are visible in the darkness of Hell, but the sun is the guide through Purgatory (see *Purgatorio* 7.44, 58; 13.17). Movement of the sun and stars also indicates a passage of time, and in this respect also Purgatory differs from Hell. There was no marking of time in Hell because there was no movement. Everyone in Hell is set in place for all eternity, without any chance of advance or fear of decline. Purgatory, by contrast, set between the timeless waste of Hell and the endless dance of Paradise, is a place where time passes and where sinners move, ascending toward the heavens.

[1] Eileen Gardiner, ed., *Visions of Heaven & Hell before Dante* (New York: Italica Press, 1989), xiii.
[2] Robin Kirkpatrick, *Dante: The Divine Comedy* (Cambridge: Cambridge University Press, 1987), 77.

Sinners in Purgatory are no less sinful than the sinners in Hell. In fact, they are often guilty of the very same sins, and at times even the punishments are similar. Dante encounters people who, especially at the bottom of the mountain, have committed great evil. Nor are the sinners in Purgatory there because they did enough good deeds to balance out their sins. The sole difference between the two is the choice of Christ. Even if conversion is secret, even if it is with the last breath, even if it is only a momentary confession of Christ, that is enough to deliver a man or woman from Hell and to place them on the fiery road to Heaven. Dante is again highlighting the importance of the human will. Those who chose evil or did not choose at all are eternally in the pit; those who use their will rightly have hope of Paradise.

At the lower levels, Purgatory is peopled with sinners who squeaked by at the last moment. Manfred, the natural son of Frederick II, who appears in canto 3, was twice excommunicated. Yet, when Dante meets him at the base of Mount Purgatory, he cheerfully explains why he is not in Hell:

> Then with a smile he said, "Manfred I am,
>   grandson of Empress Constance, and I beg you,
>   when you are with the living once again
> go to my lovely child, mother of kings
>   who honor Sicily and Aragon;
>   whatever may be rumored, tell her this:
> As I lay there, my body torn by these
>   two mortal wounds, weeping, I gave my soul
>   to Him Who grants forgiveness willingly.
> Horrible was the nature of my sins,
>   but boundless mercy stretches out its arms
>   to any man who comes in search of it.
>   (*Purgatorio* 3.112–123)

As Manfred comments, "The church's curse is not the final word/ for Everlasting Love may still return / if hope reveals the slightest hint of green" (*Purgatorio* 3.133–135). To be sure, Manfred has to endure penance for thirty times as long as he lived presumptuously, but he is saved. Similarly, Buonconte in canto 5 was saved when he "murmured Mary's name" and shed "a measly tear" (*Purgatorio* 5.101, 107).

The crucial importance of conversion is strikingly shown in the character of Statius. Though inferior to Virgil as a man and as a poet, he is higher in the afterlife, solely because he embraced Christ. This example is all the more striking because Statius became a Christian largely through the influence of Virgil. Virgil awakened poetry in him (*Purgatorio* 21.91–93), and Virgil also prepared him for Christianity. Speaking to Virgil, Statius says:

> You were the lonely traveler in the dark
> who holds his lamp behind him, shedding light
> not for himself but to make others wise;
> for you once wrote: "The world is born again;
> Justice returns, and the first age of man,
> and a new progeny descends from heaven."
> (*Purgatorio* 22.67–72)

Statius is quoting from Virgil's fourth *Eclogue*, and Statius, like many in the medieval world, sees a parallel between Virgil's words and biblical prophecies of Christ. When Statius heard Christians saying things similar to Virgil, he investigated Christian teaching and eventually was baptized. Ironically, one pagan led another pagan to Christ, and yet the first pagan remains in Hell while his convert progresses through Purgatory.

Though entry into Purgatory is purely a matter of grace and conversion, moving through Purgatory requires work and perseverance. One is not placed miraculously at the top of the mountain; one must climb. But the point is, one *can* climb. This makes "freedom" one of the key themes of Purgatory.[3] Hell is a prison (*Purgatorio* 1.41), confining people more and more tightly the lower one goes. But Dante has escaped this "eternal prison," and now he "goes in search of freedom" (*Purgatorio* 1.71). When he finally reaches the

[3] Ibid., 76.

top of the mountain, Virgil leaves him, telling him, "Now is your will upright, wholesome, and free" (*Purgatorio* 27.140).

Freedom describes a fact of human nature and also lays out a political program. Near the center of the *Purgatorio*, Marco of Lombardy discusses questions of astrology and free will with Dante. Were astrology true, he contends, human actions would be determined by the influence of the heavens, and free will would be a myth. But free will is a reality; all men are "free subjects of a greater power, / a nobler nature that creates your mind, / and over this the spheres have no control" (*Purgatorio* 16.79–81). Clearly, Dante does not see freedom and subjection as opposites. Man is free from the stars only because he is subject to the "greater power" of God. Marco admits that "the spheres initiate your tendencies," that is, they affect one's basic orientation toward life, but even then "your Free Will, which, though it may grow faint/ in its first struggles with the heavens, can still / surmount all obstacles if nurtured well" (*Purgatorio* 16.73–78). Though all men have free will, it must be "nurtured" to overcome the obstacles to freedom and to resist being enslaved.

Since freedom is a product of nurturing, men must have guides to become free. Otherwise, the soul, like a small child, will be "attracted to a trivial toy, / and though beguiled, she will run after it, / if guide or curb do not divert her love" (*Purgatorio* 16.91–93). Love and freedom are thus closely connected. Everyone seeks after what he loves, as a child is fascinated by a toy, but freedom in love is not a matter of simply following whatever one loves. True freedom arises from a love trained to love the right things. When "loves are bad" every "crooked road" is made to seem straight (*Purgatorio* 10.1–3), and one loses his way in the dark wood. Redemption thus involves a reordering of loves, so that one can act with freedom, not allowing himself to be subjected to a yoke of slavery by disordered desires.

Guides who lead others toward freedom and love must not only teach the truth but provide good examples to their disciples. Whether teachers, popes, or emperors, they must themselves act with true freedom, or else they will lead their followers astray.

People see the greed of their leaders and crave "for the same worldly goods" (*Purgatorio* 16.101). The "present state of evil in the world," Marco claims, is the rule of "bad leadership," not of "Nature that has grown corrupt in you" (*Purgatorio* 16.103–105). Only a virtuous teacher can produce free disciples, and only in a virtuous political system can anyone truly be free.

Purgatorio is a book of transitions, and these transitions operate simultaneously at several levels. Dante himself must undergo purification if he is going to be worthy of continuing his pilgrimage, and Purgatory also prepares him to be the poet and prophet of Paradise. At the same time, *Purgatorio* is laying out a pattern for all who desire to be freed for ascent to Heaven. Typically, though, Dante is concerned not only with the individual saint, but also is portraying some of the necessary steps for political renewal, for the purgation of human society. This complex process of liberation requires discipline, particularly discipline of the imagination and of desire, which are intimately connected in Dante's mind. Before looking at these themes, and the means that Dante portrays for achieving this disciplined freedom, we will take a closer look at the structure of Purgatory and the *Purgatorio*.

Mount Purgatory

Physically, Purgatory is an island mountain on the opposite side of the globe from the entrance to Hell and from Jerusalem. Terraces surround the mountain, each of which is home to the dead who are being purged of a particular sin. The terraces are connected together; so Dante's movement through Purgatory is an ascent to the top of the mountain. At the very top is the Garden of Eden, where Dante, like a new Adam, will meet his Eve, Beatrice.

Like *Inferno*, *Purgatorio* is divided into three large segments, and the divisions are marked, again like Hell, by difficult or elaborate thresholds. In cantos 1–9, Dante is in "Antepurgatory," the place where excommunicates and those who converted late in life begin their purgation. Antepurgatory is divided from Purgatory proper by a gate with three steps:

> We reached the steps. White marble was the first,
>> and polished to the glaze of a looking glass:
>> I saw myself reflected as I was.
> The second one was deeper dark than perse,
>> of four and crumbling, fire-corroded stone,
>> with cracks across its surface—length and breadth.
> The third one, lying heavy at the top,
>> appeared to be of flaming porphyry,
>> red as the blood that spurts out from a vein;
> upon this step the angel of the Lord
>> rested his feet; he sat upon the sill
>> which seemed to be of adamantine rock.
>
>   (*Purgatorio* 9.94–105)

These three entrance steps represent the three stages of repentance.[4] The first, the white step, shines like a mirror in which Dante can see himself as he really is, and thus it represents self-examination. Second is the dark step; broken and cracked, it is the step of contrition, or sorrow for sin. The final step is red like blood, but is also described as "flaming." It represents both the blood that cleanses and the flame that purges, and in a sense the third step represents the whole point of Purgatory, which is to burn away imperfections and sin. Purification begins when one sees truly, mourns over what he sees, and steps into the flames.

At the top of the stairs sits an angel who "traced upon my brow the scars of seven P's" (*Purgatorio* 9.112–113). "P" stands for *peccatum*, the Latin word for sin, and the seven P's correspond to the seven main terraces of Purgatory. Medieval theologians taught that there were seven "deadly sins," and these are represented on the seven terraces. Starting from the bottom of the mountain, with the most serious of the sins, the seven deadly sins are: pride, envy, wrath, sloth, covetousness, gluttony, and lust. As the angel tells Dante, the P's will be "cleansed away" as he makes his ascent toward the peak of the mountain (*Purgatorio* 9.113–114).

---

[4] Dorothy L. Sayers, *The Divine Comedy, II: Purgatory* (London: Penguin, 1955), 139.

The next major transition takes place in canto 27, after Dante has moved up the seven terraces of Purgatory and is ready to enter the Garden of Eden. Again he meets an angel, and again there is a difficult passage to navigate:

> It was the hour the sun's first rays shine down
> upon the land where its Creator shed
> his own life's blood, the hour the Ebro flows
> beneath high Scales, and Ganges' waters boil
> in noonday heat: so day was fading, then,
> when God's angel of joy appeared to us.
> Upon the bank beyond the fire's reach
> he stood, singing *Beati mundo corde!*
> The living beauty of his voice rang clear.
> Then: "Holy souls, no farther can you go
> without first suffering fire. So, enter now,
> and be not deaf to what is sung beyond,"
> He said to us as we came up to him.
> I, when I heard these words, felt like a man
> who is about to be entombed alive.
> Gripping my hands together, I leaned forward
> and, staring at the fire, I recalled
> what human bodies look like burned to death.
> *(Purgatorio* 27.1–18)

Noticing Dante's hesitation, Virgil reminds him of earlier difficulties that had been overcome and assures him that "if you spent/ a thousand years within the fire's heart / it would not singe a single hair of yours" (*Purgatorio* 27.25–27). Ultimately, he has to remind his disciple that "only this wall keeps you from Beatrice" (*Purgatorio* 27.36). That does the trick, and Dante enters the wall of

CANTOS	SECTION	TERRACES
1–9	Antepurgatory	1–2
Transition in canto 9		
9–27	Purgatory	3–9
Transition in canto 27		
27–33	Eden	peak

flame, whose intensity is like "the depths of boiling glass" (*Purgatorio* 27.50). Dante thinks of himself as one "entombed alive," and the wall of flame reminds him of bodies "burned to death." Yet he must be willing to suffer this death in order to receive the blessing that is being sung on the other side, the blessing that comes to the "pure of heart" who will "see God."

Thus these two thresholds mark out the structure for Purgatory. Notice again the prominence of nine-fold structures. As in Hell, there are nine main sections, two of Antepurgatory and the seven terraces in Purgatory itself. Moreover, the first transition takes place in canto 9; it is followed by 18 cantos (2 x 9) describing Dante's journey through Purgatory. Finally, the ascent from Purgatory to Eden takes place in canto 27 (3 x 9).

Three dreams also function structurally in *Purgatorio*. Dante's first dream takes place in canto 9, before he comes to the three steps:

> dreaming, I seemed to see hovering above,
>   a golden-feathered eagle in the sky,
>   with wings outspread, and ready to swoop down . . . .
> Dreaming, I saw him circle for a while,
>   then terrible as lightning, he struck down,
>   swooping me up, up to the sphere of fire.
> And there it seemed the bird and I both burned;
>   the heat of that imaginary blaze
>   was so intense it woke me from my sleep.
>   (*Purgatorio* 9.19–21, 28–33)

When he awakes, Virgil explains that while he slept a lady came, St. Lucy, who carried Dante to the entrance of Purgatory. Dante's dream of an eagle was fulfilled in reality in Lucy. Eagles will appear again near the end of *Purgatorio*, in part as a representation of Dante's own soaring poetic gifts. He strives to be like Homer, "the master singer of sublimest verse, / who soars above all others like the eagle" (*Inferno* 4.95–96).[5] In this first dream, the eagle

---

[5] See Peter Dronke, *Dante and Medieval Latin Traditions* (Cambridge: Cambridge University Press, 1986), 65.

probably functions on this level too. Not only Lucy, but the eagle of Dante's muse, brings Dante to the threshold of Purgatory.

The appearance of Lucy links *Purgatorio* with *Inferno*. St. Lucy and Beatrice sent help to Dante in the dark wood, and now as he enters Purgatory, he again receives help from St. Lucy. When Dante completes his journey to the top of Mount Purgatory, he encounters Beatrice again. Purgatory is a part of a grand love poem, worthy of "she who makes blessed."

Dante's second dream is of "a woman, stuttering / cross-eyed, stumbling along on her maimed feet, with ugly yellow skin and hands deformed" (*Purgatorio* 19.7–9). As Dante stares at her, she straightens, her stammering tongue is loosed, and she begins to sing like one of the sirens who enticed Ulysses' ships toward the rocky shore. Dante is captivated by her song so that his mind is unable to draw away. But he is rescued when a "saintly lady" appears. Virgil fixes his eyes on the lady, and then "seized the other, ripped her garment off / exposing her as far down as the paunch! / The stench pouring from her woke me from sleep" (*Purgatorio* 19.31–33). This dream illustrates a theme already introduced by the episode of Francesca de Rimini, namely, the role of imagination in sin. The woman whom Dante sees in the dream is not attractive in herself; she becomes attractive because Dante's eyes work on her "like the sun revives a body numbed by night's cold" and because "her tongue was loosened by my gaze" (*Purgatorio* 19.10–11, 16). As Dante began to learn in Hell, living virtuously means seeing things as they really are. He is learning in Purgatory that seeing rightly requires discipline of the imagination.

Dante's final dream takes place in canto 27, after he has passed through the fire that separates Purgatory from Eden at the top:

> I dreamed I saw a young and lovely girl
> walking within a meadow picking flowers;
> and, as she moved along, she sang these words:
> "If anyone should want to know my name,
> I am called Leah. And I spend all my time

> weaving garlands of flowers with my fair hands,
> to please me when I stand before my mirror;
> my sister Rachel sits all the day long
> before her own and never moves away.
> She loves to contemplate her lovely eyes;
> I love to use my hands to adorn myself:
> her joy is in reflection, mine in act."
>
> (*Purgatorio* 27.97–108)

Rachel and Leah, the two daughters of Laban and wives of Jacob, were understood in medieval times as representatives of two ways of life. Leah represents the "active" life of work and public involvement, while Rachel represents the contemplative life of prayer and meditation. This dream, in contrast to the dream of the siren, leads Dante to those things that can bring true satisfaction, action and contemplation.

Putting the dreams together with the transitions, we find that *Purgatorio* is arranged chiastically:

Antepurgatory, 1–8
  Dream, Lucy, 9
    Entry to purgatory, 9
      Purgatory: 10–18 (9 cantos)
        Dream of the siren, canto 19
      Purgatory, 19–27 (9 cantos)
    Exit to Paradise, 27
  Dream of Leah and Rachel, 27
Earthly Paradise, 28–33

Numerically, the central canto in *Purgatorio* is canto 17, with sixteen cantos on either side. Significantly, canto 17 is devoted to Virgil's explanation of the moral structure of Purgatory.[6] The

---

[6] The structural importance of canto 17 is marked out by other patterns. The number of lines in each canto is not uniform, but it occasionally falls into patterns. The central eleven books of *Purgatorio* (12–22) follow this pattern in numbers of lines: 136, 154, 151, 145, 145, 139, 145, 145, 151, 136, 154. The two books at each end of this sequence have the same number of lines in the same order, and within this "bracket," the number of lines is arranged chiastically (ABBCBBA). Significantly, the central canto of the sequence is canto 17.

terraces of Antepurgatory are outside the discussion, but they are home to those who were excommunicated but repented at some late date, and to those who died without confession, without being "shriven." In canto 17, Virgil is concerned with the levels of Purgatory proper.

In the background is Augustine's distinction between "things to be used" and "things to be enjoyed," which he develops in his treatise *On Christian Teaching* (*de doctrina Christiana*). According to Augustine, to "enjoy" something is to love it and delight in it for its own sake. Given this definition, he concludes that God alone is to be enjoyed. To enjoy a created thing is to make it into an idol, a replacement for God. Everything other than God is to be loved or enjoyed not for its own sake, but for the sake of God. For Augustine, directing one's love and desire toward anything other than God is of the essence of sin. Along with Augustine, Dante is drawing on Aristotle. Aristotle taught a "teleological" view of the world, the idea that everything in the world seeks a particular end or goal that is suited to the nature of the thing. Flame moves up because fire is a light element, and thus it seeks its proper place in the sky. Man also moves toward an end, the goal of happiness, which is suited to the nature of humanity as a rational and social animal. Add a pinch of Augustine and a dash of Aristotle and you get Dante's theory that everything moves toward the end or goal that is determined by the object of its love.

As Virgil points out, whatever we do, we do for love of something. So long as our love is directed to the right object, love is the "seed of every virtue growing in you" (*Purgatorio* 17.104). Love can, however, be misdirected, and thereby it becomes the seed of "every deed that merits punishment." Since love cannot ignore itself, nothing can hate itself, and since everything exists only because of its connection with God, "no creature has the power to hate his God" (*Purgatorio* 17.111). Biblically, this is not correct, for some men do hate God. Here as in other places in Dante, Aristotle overwhelms Paul.

According to Virgil, love can be misdirected in three ways. Sins that involve love for evil things are the worst sorts of sins.

Some people, for example, believe that they can rise only if others fall. Their desire for success is at the same time a desire for their neighbors' failure. This is Virgil's description of "pride," the first of the seven deadly sins and the one represented by the first terrace of Purgatory. Envy is the second form of loving evil. Some people fear losing honor and fame and want to be superior to everyone, and therefore they are vexed by a neighbor's good fortune. Like the prideful, the envious wish the worst for their neighbors. The third terrace is the terrace of the wrathful, who, by seeking revenge and by flaring up in rage, also seek evil.

Even love for what is good can be sinful. To understand this, we need to again introduce a concept from Aristotle. According to Aristotle, virtue, doing the good, always means finding the middle ground between two extremes. Courage, for example, is a virtue that stands between cowardice and foolishness. Cowardice is a vice because it is a "defect" of courage; a coward is someone who does not have enough spirit to be courageous. Foolhardiness, by contrast, is also a vice, because it is excessive. A foolish person has too much spirit; though his actions look courageous, they are not. True courage is the "golden mean" between the defect of cowardice and the excess of folly. Virgil reflects this ethical scheme when he describes the moral structure of the final four terraces of Purgatory. None of the sinners on these terraces loved evil. They all loved the good, but they loved it either defectively or excessively. Defective love of the good translates into sloth or laziness. The slothful grasp at the good, but with lukewarm love, and therefore they cannot reach it. Achieving a good requires effort, but the slothful are unwilling to expend themselves. The rest of the terraces are concerned with "love that without measure pursues its good." Money and material wealth are, for Dante, goods. But an excessive love for this good is a vice, the vice of "avarice" or "greed." Food and drink are goods, but excessive devotion to food and drink is gluttony, the sin of the eighth terrace of Purgatory. Sex is a good, but excessive devotion to sex is the sin of lust.

Purgatory, it should be seen, has the same moral geography as Hell. In both, sins of the flesh, sins of incontinence, are the least serious types of sins, and in both, deliberate love of evil is the worst sort of sin. In both, the lesser sinners are physically "higher" than the more serious sinners. Lust is punished in the second circle of Hell, near the top of the pit, and lust is purged in the ninth terrace of Purgatory. Turn Mount Purgatory upside down and insert it into Hell, and the two would match almost completely, terrace to circle.

Review Questions

1. Explain the symbolism of light and movement in *Purgatorio*.
2. What kind of sinners are in Antepurgatory?
3. What does Dante mean by "freedom"? How is it related to the purification that takes place in Purgatory?
4. Describe the physical appearance of Purgatory.
5. Explain the threefold structure of *Purgatorio*.
6. What do the steps that lead into Purgatory represent?
7. What do the seven "P's" on Dante's forehead signify?
8. What is the significance of Dante's dream of the siren in *Purgatorio* 19?
9. Explain the moral structure of Purgatory.
10. What is the "golden mean"?

Thought Questions

1. How does climbing Mount Purgatory differ from climbing other mountains? (*Purgatorio* 4.88–96). How does this fit into Dante's conception of Hell and Purgatory?
2. What are the three groups of the "late repentant"?
3. What does Dante see in *Purgatorio* 8.97–108? What is the significance of this episode?
4. Who appears to Dante and Virgil as they move from the terrace of wrath? (*Purgatorio* 17.40–63) Why is this significant at this point?

hell = circles
purgatory = terraces

Disciplines of Purity

Though the gracious forgiveness of God is the key to getting into Purgatory, Purgatory is a journey that demands self-discipline in the formation of virtue. Already in the first canto, this feature of Purgatory is highlighted. As Dante surveys the sky from the bottom of the mountain, he sees "those four stars / the first man saw, and no man after him" (*Purgatorio* 1.23–24). The four stars represent the four cardinal virtues: prudence, temperance, justice, and fortitude.[7] The "widowed" North is deprived of the sight of these stars, not because no one possesses the virtues, but because they are not a natural sight, nor available to everyone. Seeing these stars at the beginning of the journey gives a clue to the goal of the journey: growth in these virtues. As always, Dante is making his way toward light.

Another clue to the meaning of Purgatory is offered by the gatekeeper:

> I saw near me an ancient man, alone,
>> whose face commanded all the reverence
>> that any son could offer to his sire.
> Long-flowing was his beard and streaked with white,
>> as was his hair, which in two tresses fell
>> to rest upon his chest on either side.
> The rays of light from these four sacred stars
>> struck with such radiance upon his face,
>> it was as if the sun were shining there.
>
> (Purgatorio1.31–39)

The "ancient man" is the Roman Cato, a Stoic pagan who chose to kill himself rather than accept Caesar's victory in Rome. Why is Cato the guardian of Purgatory? No doubt Cato represented for Dante the heights of pagan virtue, resulting from the severe self-control of the Stoic. Cato is a fitting guardian for Purgatory because the "four stars" shine in his face like the sun. The goal of

---

[7] Sayers, *Purgatory*, 77–78.

Purgatory is to make the same stars shine in the face of every sinner.

Dante's progression from one terrace to another follows a fairly fixed pattern. We can examine his entrance to the first terrace of Purgatory proper to illustrate (canto 10). Standing on the terrace, Dante looks at the cliff face of the mountain, which

> was pure white marble; on its flawless face
> > were carvings that would surely put to shame
> > not only Polyclete but Nature too.
> The angel who came down to announce on earth
> > the peace longed for by weeping centuries,
> > which broke the ancient ban and opened Heaven,
> appeared before our eyes: a shape alive,
> > carved in an attitude of marble grace,
> > an effigy that could have spoken words.
> One would have sworn he was saying "Ave!"
> > for she who turned the key, opening for us
> > the Highest Love, was also figured there;
> the outlines of her image carved the words
> > *Ecce ancilla Dei*, as clearly cut
> > as is the imprint of a seal on wax.
> > > > (*Purgatorio* 10.31–45)

Looking past this scene, another appears:

> Carved in the spread of marble there, I saw
> > the cart and oxen with the holy Ark:
> > a warning not to exceed one's competence.
> Ahead of it moved seven separate choirs
> > testing my senses: one of these said, "No,"
> > the other one said, "Yes, they truly sing!"
> With equal art, the smoke which censers poured
> > was traced so faithfully that eyes and nose
> > could not decide between a "yes" or "no."

Ahead, and far beyond the sacred Ark,
   his robes girt up, the humble Psalmist danced,
   showing himself both more and less than king.
Depicted on the other side was Michal,
   as from a palace window she looked on
   her face revealed her sadness and her scorn.
                        (*Purgatorio* 10.55–69)

Scenes from history follow, but these are enough to give an idea
of what is going on. The first scene is, of course, Gabriel's annuncia-
tion to Mary concerning the birth of Jesus. It also records Mary's
response, in Latin, "Behold the handmaiden of God" (Lk. 1:26–38).
The second carving depicts two scenes from 2 Samuel 6, both having to do with the entry of the ark of the covenant into Jerusalem.
In the first, Dante sees Uzzah, the man who died when he touched
the ark to keep it from tipping over; he takes it as a "warning not to
exceed one's competence." In the second, David is dancing before
the ark as it enters the city, while his wife Michal, Saul's daughter,
watches the king's humility with horror and scorn.

All of these scenes illustrate either pride, the vice that is being
purged in the first terrace, or its opposite. Mary and David both
respond to God with humility, but Uzzah and Michal are, in their
different ways, prideful. Uzzah touches the ark he has no right to
touch, and Michal's haughtiness leads her to despise David in her
heart. Viewing these examples of virtue and vice, Dante's imagination is already beginning to be cleansed. Art, including Dante's own
poem, is an aid in sanctification.

Art has an important role in Purgatory because what must especially be disciplined are sight and imagination. Dante's imagination
must be cleansed if he is to be worthy to record his experiences in
poetry. Imagination has a central role in sin because imagination
can so easily lead to false vision, as the dream of the siren in canto
19 illustrates. Dante even goes so far as to suggest that imagination
endows things with lovable qualities. The Siren is no beauty; Dante's
imagination makes her beautiful.

Prior to this dream, Virgil has been instructing Dante on the nature of desire. Souls are "created quick to love" and "will move toward anything that pleases it, / as soon as pleasure causes it to move" (*Purgatorio* 18.19–21). The interaction between love and imagination begins when we perceive a real object, say, a gold necklace. From that real object, "apprehensive power / extracts an image it displays within you." That is to say, even when we are not looking at the gold necklace, we retain its image within us. Armed with this "image," we can "imagine" what it would be like to wear the necklace, to be admired for it, to dazzle everyone with it.

As we direct attention to the imagined necklace, we incline toward it, and "that inclination is love" (*Purgatorio* 18.22–27). Virgil explains further by comparing desire to a flame:

> Just as a fire's flames always rise up,
> inspired by its own nature to ascend,
> seeking to be in its own element,
> just so, the captive soul begins its quest,
> the spiritual movement of its love,
> not resting till the thing loved is enjoyed.
> It should be clear to you by now how blind
> to truth those people are who make the claims
> that every love is, in itself, good love.
> They think this, for love's substance, probably,
> seems always good, but though the wax is good,
> the impression made upon it may be bad.
> (*Purgatorio* 18.28–39)

Whether love is good or bad then depends entirely on whether or not it is inclined toward a good thing or an evil thing, and particularly whether it is inclined to a good or bad image. If our imaginations form images that are false, our love will be wrongly directed. If our imaginations are full of evil, then our love will be enslaved. If, on the other hand, our imaginations are full of truth, the truth will set us free. With the example of the gold necklace, the question is whether the inclination of our imagination is excessive. Gold necklaces are good in themselves, but if our imagination endows them with too much value, our love for them will be evil.

We will have become covetous. Things we love impress themselves on the "wax" of our love; they form love into its own shape. For this reason, we must be very careful about what kinds of things we allow to impress themselves on our "wax."

Consistent with this emphasis on imagination, the rebirth occurring in Purgatory also involves the rebirth of poetry and art: "Here let death's poetry arise to life," Dante prays as he begins the canticle (*Purgatorio* 1.7). Fittingly, many poets and artists are in Purgatory or mentioned there, and as Dante progresses through Purgatory a community of poets is formed, stretching from Virgil, the pagan poet who prepares the way for the Christian Statius, to Dante and the poets of his time. Art is a part of the restoration of moral imagination, and one of the means for that restoration.

Yet art alone is not enough to ascend to Paradise. It is an ennobling pursuit that restores certain virtues but not a salvific enterprise. Art can even be a distraction from the pursuit of holiness, a point symbolized early in the canticle. At the base of the mountain, Dante meets his friend Casella, a Florentine musician. Dante asks Casella to sing, and the song is so sweet that for a moment it seems that the music is all that exists. Cato interrupts Dante's aesthetic ecstasy, for the rigor of the mountain does not allow for indulgence in artistic pleasures for their own sake (*Purgatorio* 2.119–123). Art, in Augustinian terms, is a thing to be used rather than enjoyed.

Other goods must also be renounced if Dante is going to make it to the peak of Purgatory. Virgil, for example, is finally left behind, not because he or what he represents is evil but because it has limited value. Similarly, various kings appear in Antepurgatory, sent there because they have devoted themselves to politics and have been negligent of more important pursuits (*Purgatorio* 7.103, 121). Dante also comments on the limitations of family and kinship connections. Sap, he says, rarely rises to all the branches, and in the same way not all the members of the family receive the invigorating power of the roots. Good things like a family name can even be turned to evil, as Omberto Aldobrandesco points out (*Purgatorio* 11.58–72). Later in the same canticle, Oderisi, a manuscript illuminator, warns that fame is fleeting like grass (*Purgatorio* 11.115). In Purgatory, all human pursuits and all human goods are subordinated to the quest for salvation.

Many of the terraces begin with Mary as a counterexample of the vice being purged. As Dante reaches the second terrace, he hears a voice saying *"Vinum non habent,"* "They have no wine" (*Purgatorio* 13.29), the words that Mary speaks to Jesus at the wedding of Cana (Jn. 2:3). This appears at the beginning of the terrace of envy, and it shows that Mary manifested the opposing virtue of generosity. At the terrace of the wrathful, Mary is seen whispering "tenderly as a mother would, 'My son / why hast Thou dealt with us this way? You see / Thy father and I, both of us in tears, have searched for Thee'" (*Purgatorio* 15.89–92). The scene is from Luke 2, when Jesus is missing after Passover and Mary and Joseph go searching for him throughout Jerusalem, finally discovering him in the temple. Mary, the model of all virtue, reacts with tender questions, not raging demands. As he enters the terrace of the slothful, Dante hears a voice quoting Luke 2:39: "Mary in haste ran to the hills" (*Purgatorio* 18.100). Mary has a prominent role in the *Purgatorio*. Mainly she is the model of all Christian virtue rather than some kind of redemptive agent in herself.

Exits from the terraces are also similar. Again, we can examine the first terrace as an example (canto 12). As Dante passes on from the terrace of the prideful, he sees still more carvings on the wall. In this case they include Satan, Briareus (one of the giants who challenged Jupiter), and Nimrod, alternating classical and biblical examples of the proud who have been brought low. The relief carvings thus not only provide examples of virtue and vice, but also show something of the final result of vice. His exit is accompanied by music, the singing of *Beati pauperes spiritu*, "Blessed are the poor in spirit," the first of the Beatitudes (Mt. 5). The Beatitude is an appropriate choice, since poverty of spirit is the opposite of pride. Dante's exits from the other terraces are likewise accompanied by the singing of an appropriate Beatitude.

Another thing happens at each exit:

As we were climbing up the sacred steps,
   I seemed to feel myself much lighter now
   than I had been before on level ground.
"Master," I said, "tell me, what heavy thing
   has been removed from me? I feel as if
   to keep on climbing would be effortless."
He answered, "When the P's that still remain
   (Though they have almost faded) on your brow
   shall be erased completely like the first,
then will your feet be light with good desire;
   they will no longer feel the heavy road
   but will rejoice as they are urged to climb."
Then I did something anyone might do,
   made conscious by the way men looked at him
   that he must have some strange thing on his head:
his hand will try hard to investigate,
   feeling around to find, fulfilling thus
   the duty that the eyes cannot perform;
so, my right hand with fingers spread found just
   six of the seven letters that were carved
   upon my brow by him who keeps the keys.
Observing this, my master smiled at me.
                 (*Purgatorio* 12.115–136)

The "P" of pride has been purged, and the ascent toward Eden becomes easier. At the exit of each terrace another P is removed, and Dante gets even lighter.[8]

Dante not only undergoes purification himself, but he witnesses the purification of others. This furthers his education in virtue that began in Hell. One of the key things he learns is the importance of discipline. Discipline is applied either by forcing sinners to endure the effects of their sin or forcing them to tame and control their

---

[8] One thing is unique to this terrace: In 12 tercets of canto 12 (from lines 25–60), the opening letters to the tercet are significant. The first four begin with "u" (or "v"), the next four with "o," and the last four with "m." Dante thus forms an acrostic with "uom," the Italian word for "man." Pride is, for Dante, so characteristically human that his poem on pride forms the letters of the word "man."

sinful appetites. The envious in terrace 2, for example, have their eyes sewn shut "with iron threads, like falcons newly caught / whose eyes we stitch to tame their restlessness" (*Purgatorio* 13.71–72). Here the discipline fits the sin. In life, the envious could not look on joy without feeling pangs of resentment, and therefore they are now prevented from looking at anything. Deprived of sight, Purgatory will "tame their restlessness." The wrathful are enclosed in thick smoke. Here, the purgation takes place not by preventing the exercise of vice but by forcing the sinner to confront the effects of his sin. Dante himself realizes that the smoke might lead to violence:

> Just as the blind man walks close to his guide
> > in order not to stray, or to collide
> > with something that could hurt or even kill him,
> so I moved through that foul and acrid air,
> > hearing my guide keep telling me: "Watch out!
> > Be very careful not to lose me here."
> > > > (*Purgatorio* 16.10–15)

Penance sometimes takes the form of practicing the virtue that is the opposite of the vice being punished. The slothful, for instance, are forced to run swiftly around the cornice shouting out in praise of zealous acts and people (canto 18). They are required to exercise the zeal they never displayed in life. Gluttony is disciplined in a similar way:

> But then, right in the road a tree appeared,
> > laden with fruit whose fragrance filled the air,
> > and instantly that pleasant talk was stopped!
> Just as a fir tree tapers toward the top
> > from branch to branch, so this one tapered down,
> > to keep the souls from climbing, I suppose.
> On that side where our way was bounded,
> > poured clear water from the high rock to the tree,
> > sprinkling the topmost leaves in its cascade.
> As the two poets drew close, there came a voice

that shouted at us from within the tree:
"This fruit and water is denied to you."
(*Purgatorio* 22.130–141)

Liturgical discipline is also involved. Singing, chanting, and prayer are offered according to the sin. The wrathful sing the *Agnus Dei* ("Lamb of God") in praise of the meek Savior (*Purgatorio* 16.18), while the gluttonous sing *"labina mea domine"* (*Purgatorio* 23.11), a quotation from Psalm 51:15 that asks God to open their mouths in praise rather than for food. Meanwhile, the lustful sing *Summae Deus Clementiae*, "God of Supreme Clemency," a prayer for release from the power of lust (*Purgatorio* 25.121). Learning to sing of Christian virtues is one way of learning to embody those virtues. When we have learned to sing, we will become the song.

Purgation is not only for the individual; it also has political and social dimensions. If, as Dante has shown in *Inferno*, sin rends community and disrupts the city, then Purgatory must heal community and prepare souls for the eternal dance of Paradise. Consistent with this, there are many reunions in Purgatory and more hugging than a family reunion. In canto 2, Dante sees his friend Casella and tries three times to embrace him (*Purgatorio* 2.76–81). In canto 7, we meet Rudolf and Ottokar (*Purgatorio* 7.91–102). Rudolf was elected in 1273 to be Emperor, but Ottokar opposed him and was finally defeated and killed in 1278. Now, in Purgatory, Rudolf is comforted by Ottokar; they are political rivals turned into brothers. Even Virgil is reunited with old friends. Virgil speaks only the word "Mantua," and Sordello, another Italian poet, embraces him (*Purgatorio* 6.67). Hell, like Marvell's "grave," is a "fine and private place, / but none, I think, do there embrace." But Purgatory, that's a different story.

Dante launches into a lengthy diatribe about the strife that besets Italy as the embrace of the two poets displays the kind of union that should characterize his land. The invective against Italy points to two main reasons for the corruption of Italy. First are the "priests" who "should pursue your holiness" but instead seek to take

Hell = individuality — circles
Purgation = community — terraces
Paradise — enlightenment, spheres
love
REDEEMED FROM FIRE BY FIRE   127

over Caesar's saddle. This leads to disaster, Dante announces to the priests: "see how this beast [of empire] has grown viciously wild, / without the rider's spurs to set her straight, / since you dared take the reigns into your hands" (*Purgatorio* 6.91–96). Alongside the usurping priests, Dante condemns the irresponsible emperors:

> O German Albert, you abandon her,
>   allowing her, ungoverned, to run wild.
>   You should have been astride the saddle-bow!
> Let a just judgment fall down from the stars
>   upon your house: one unmistakable
>   and strange enough to terrify your heir!
> You and your sire, whom greed for greater wealth
>   holds back up there, have let this come to pass:
>   the garden of the Empire is laid waste .
>   (*Purgatorio* 6. 97–105)

What was once a new Eden has become a wasteland. If priests and emperors were purged of greed and sloth, Eden would be renewed.

Many readers find *Purgatorio* less interesting than *Inferno*, and in part this is because Purgatory lacks the colorful characters and memorable scenes of horror that are found throughout Hell. There are no Ulysses or Francescas, individual personalities who dominate entire cantos. But this is not a failure of imagination on Dante's part; it is a deliberate thematic device. For Dante, individuality is not itself praiseworthy. In truth, the fact that the sinners in Hell stand out from all others is a part of their damnation. Hell is a place of individuals, while Purgatory is the beginning of community. Jean-Paul Sartre said, *"L'enfer, c'est les autres"*—"Hell is other people." Dante might say, *"L'enfer, c'est moi seul"*—"Hell is myself alone."

Review Questions

1. What do the four stars in canto 1 represent? What does this tell us about Purgatory as a whole?

2. Who is Cato? Why is he the guardian of Purgatory?

3. What is the function of art in Purgatory?

4. Explain the links between sense, imagination, and love. What is Dante trying to teach us with this discussion?

5. How does Mary the mother of Jesus fit into Dante's purposes in Purgatory?

6. What happens as Dante leaves a particular terrace of Purgatory?

7. What is the logic behind the "punishments" of those who are in Purgatory?

8. Give some examples of how Purgatory is a place of social and political renewal.

Thought Questions

1. What does Guido del Duca say in the terrace of envy? (*Purgatorio* 14.22–66). Does Dante agree with this?

2. What Beatitude is sung in the terrace of wrath? (*Purgatorio* 17.68–69) Why?

3. Describe the exemplars mentioned in the circle of sloth, and explain how they symbolize this vice or the opposing virtue (*Purgatorio* 18.100–102)

4. Why is there an earthquake as Dante walks along the terrace of greed? (*Purgatorio* 21.40–72)

5. How has Forese Donati been able to ascend from Ante-purgatory to the terrace of gluttony? (*Purgatorio* 23.76–114) What conclusions does Forese draw from this?

6. Who are the exemplars of chastity for the lustful? (*Purgatorio* 25.127–132)

New Adam and New Eve

Once Dante has passed through the wall of fire into the Garden of Eden, he stands beside the river Lethe and watches a magnificent parade. At the head of the procession are "four-and-twenty elders, two by two, / all of them wearing crowns of fleur-de-lis" and singing a hymn of blessing to the one who is most blessed "of all of Adam's daughters." Four six-winged creatures follow, covered with eyes and each wearing a crown "of forest green." The four creatures stand in a square, and within the square is a chariot "drawn by a griffon." Near the right wheel are "three ladies circling in a dance," one red, one emerald green, the other white as "new-fallen snow." On the opposite side, near the left wheel, are four more ladies "dressed in purple robes, and led by one with three eyes in her head." Behind the dancers are two old men, one dressed as "a follower of great Hippocrates," and the other carrying "a sword, so sharp, gleaming so bright / that I, though on the other bank, felt fear." Four men came next, and then "an old man, by himself, / who moved in his own dream, his face inspired" (*Purgatorio* 29.82–153).

The whole pageant is an allegorical representation of the history of salvation. The twenty-four elders are the twelve patriarchs and the twelve apostles, and Dante explicitly refers to the visions of Ezekiel to explain the meaning of the four winged creatures (*Purgatorio* 29.100–102). Griffons, as composite beasts (bird and lion), frequently represent the God-man. It is the "beast who in two natures is one single being" (*Purgatorio* 31.80–81). The ladies who dance around the Christ-drawn chariot represent the virtues, the four "natural" virtues of courage, prudence, justice, and temperance, and the three "theological" virtues of faith, hope, and love. One of the old men who follows is Luke, dressed in the garb of Hippocrates, the Greek physician, for Luke, according to Paul, was a physician (Col. 4:14). Accompanying Luke is Paul himself, carrying the frightful sword of the Word of God. The four humble men who come next represent the writers of the minor epistles: James, Peter, John, and Jude, and in the train of the procession is the apostle John, the John of the Book of Revelation, moving, like Dante himself, "in his own dream."

All this leads us to expect an appearance of Christ as the central figure of the Bible and of salvation history. As the parade stops in front of Dante, song breaks out, and the expectation is heightened. One of the twenty-four sings *Veni, sponsa, di Libano*, "Come, bride, from Lebanon," a quotation from the Song of Songs (4:8) that medieval writers would normally have interpreted as a reference to the church. In response, "a hundred spirits" begin throwing flowers in the air and shouting, *Benedictus qui venis*, "Blessed are you who comes," the song of welcome to Jesus at Palm Sunday, when he rode into Jerusalem on a donkey (*Purgatorio* 30.10–21). As the lilies shower around, Dante hears a quotation from Virgil: *Manibus, O, date lilia plenis*—"O, give us lilies with full hands" (*Purgatorio* 30.21). This line appears in Book 6 of the *Aeneid*, the book in which Aeneas is traveling to the underworld. His father, Anchises, is telling him about the glorious future of Rome, but the pageant of Roman history ends on a sorrowful note, describing the death of Marcellus, the nephew and intended heir of Augustus Caesar, who died at the young age of twenty-one. Lilies are strewn on his grave. In Virgil, the lilies are a sign of mourning for the dead; in Dante, the line becomes part of a celebration. But it also sounds a more somber note, as if this celebration too might end at a grave.

If we are expecting Christ, however, our expectations are frustrated:

> even so, within a nebula of flowers
>   that flowed upward from angels' hands and then
>   poured down, covering all the chariot,
> appeared a lady—over her white veil
>   an olive crown and, under her green cloak,
>   her gown, the color of eternal flame.
> And instantly—though many years had passed
>   since last I stood trembling before her eyes,
>   captured by adoration, stunned by awe—
> my soul, that could not see her perfectly,
>   still felt, succumbing to her mystery
>   and power, the strength of its enduring love.
>   (*Purgatorio* 30.28–39)

Where we expect an appearance of Christ, Dante gives us Beatrice, dressed in a crown and robes whose colors match those of the theological virtues. For Dante, she is at the center of redemptive history. Again, he surely does not intend to displace Christ from the center. Rather, he praises Beatrice as the "one who makes blessed," the agent by which the grace of Christ came to him and gave him new life. But it is hard to read this praise without feeling that Dante is less a worshiper of Christ than of his beloved.

Dante's expectations are frustrated as much as ours. He has gone through Hell to reach Beatrice, and he has just stepped through the wall of flame. He is in Eden, a new Adam ready to meet his Eve. You would think she would appreciate all he has been through, and all for *her*. Not a chance. Her first words are a sharp rebuke: "Yes, look at me! Yes, I am Beatrice! / So, you at last have deigned to climb the mount? / You learned at last that here lies human bliss?" (*Purgatorio* 30.73–75). Like a "guilty child facing his mother," Dante stands abject and begins to weep, while Beatrice tells the others in the procession that "my purpose is / to make the one who weeps on that far bank / perceive the truth and match his guilt with grief" (*Purgatorio* 30.106–108). Her specific charge is that "when I passed into my second age / and changed my life for Life, that man you see / strayed after others and abandoned me" (*Purgatorio* 30.124–126), and thus he "wandered from the path that leads to truth, / pursuing simulacra of the good, / which promise more than they can ever give" (*Purgatorio* 30.130–132). Dante's love has been directed to others, and Beatrice is not amused. From Beatrice's angle, Dante's descent to Hell was the only medicine strong enough to save his soul. But even passing through Hell is not enough, for no one may pass through the river of Lethe, the river of forgetfulness that leads to heavenly bliss, without first repenting: "penitence poured forth in guilty tears" is the ticket to cross the river (*Purgatorio* 30.144). If Dante was expecting a welcoming embrace from his Penelope, he is disappointed. This is not really a reunion of lovers. For Dante, it is Judgment Day.

Then Beatrice turns directly to Dante and challenges him: "what appealed to you, what did you find / so promising in all those other things / that made you feel obliged to spend your time / in courting them?" (*Purgatorio* 31.28–31). Confronted with her question, Dante can do nothing but confess that he has devoted himself to things that do not last: "Those things with their false joys, / offered me by the world, led me astray / when I no longer saw your countenance" (*Purgatorio* 31.33–36). This confession is the means by which Dante is spared before Beatrice, his judge; confession allows the "grind-stone" to be turned "back against the blade," blunting the sword of justice so that the sentence is not carried out. But Beatrice is not finished with Dante, for she goes on to tell him the lesson that he *should* have learned from her death:

> You never saw in Nature or in Art
> > a beauty like the beauty of my form,
> > > which clothed me once and now is turned to dust;
> and if that perfect beauty disappeared
> > when I departed from this world, how could
> > another mortal object lure your love?
> > > > > > (*Purgatorio* 31.49–54)

Beatrice's death should have encouraged Dante to seek joy, love, and satisfaction in that which cannot be changed and cannot die. He should have learned to distinguish, like Augustine, between that which can be used and that which can be enjoyed.

The fact that the whole pageant climaxes with Dante's repentance shows that there is an interplay between the historical and the personal throughout this section of *Purgatorio*. The chariot represents not only the church, but Dante's own soul, and the griffon represents something like Dante's poetic genius. Dante's surname, Alighieri, means "winged," and there are several winged creatures in this scene—not only the griffon, but the eagle, and even Dante himself, for Beatrice tells him that "No pretty girl or any other brief / attraction should have weighed down your wings" (*Purgatorio* 31.59; see *Inferno* 4.95–96). From this perspective, it is no accident that Beatrice is riding in the chariot, for she is the *anima* (soul) that first animated him. Beatrice's rebuke also becomes clearer from this perspective: She is berating him for misusing his poetic gifts and being attracted to other sources of inspiration. He must repent if he is going to be prepared for the poetic heights of *Paradiso*.[9]

Only after he has confessed is he ready to see the future, the vision that Beatrice shows him. Dante has fallen asleep under the tree of the knowledge of good and evil, which the griffon has brought to bloom, and when he awakes he finds that he is alone with Beatrice. At her direction, he watches the chariot and sees a series of events: first an eagle, moving like lightning, "swooped down / and through the tree, tearing off newborn leaves, / rending the bark, destroying all the blooms." With the branches of the tree, the eagle "struck the chariot, / which staggered like a ship caught in a storm, / careened by waves, tilting starboard and port" (*Purgatorio* 32.109–117). Eagles adorned the standards of the Roman army, and this eagle, called "the bird of Jove," represents Rome. His attack on the chariot is an attack on the church, and this allegory points to the Roman persecution of Christians in the early centuries of the church. The tree is the tree of knowledge, which has been revived by the griffon (*Purgatorio* 32.37–60), and the fact that the eagle lacerates it suggests that the attack on the church is like another fall of man, another stripping of the trees of Eden. Christ's "ship," a new Noah's ark, is tossed by the eagle's strike, but it is not overturned. The chariot survives the furious persecution of Rome.

No sooner has the chariot-ship righted itself than Dante sees "Into the cradle of the glorious care . . . a fox leap up, so lean it seemed/ the food it fed on had no nourishment" (*Purgatorio* 32.119–120). Beatrice is able to chase the fox away, "accusing it of foul abominations" (*Purgatorio* 32.123). Foxes are legendary deceivers and tricksters, overcoming their enemies not with superior power but with wit and cunning. The eagle represented Rome's direct confrontation with the church, but the fox actually gets into the chariot and attempts to turn it from its course. It represents

---

[9] See Dronke, *Dante and Medieval Latin Traditions*, chapter 3.

heresy, the attack on the church from within. A similar sequence
is found in Revelation 12. When the Christ child is born to the
woman clothed with the sun, the dragon launches a direct attack
upon him. This attack fails when the child is caught up to heaven
to make war against the dragon, but the dragon mounts another
attack, this time on the woman, with water that flows from his
mouth. Water from the mouth is a symbol of teaching, and the
dragon is trying to drown the woman and overcome the church
through false doctrine. Again, however, the Lord intervenes to
rescue, and the earth opens up to swallow the flow of water from
the dragon's mouth.

After the fox's infiltration of the chariot, the eagle returns. This
time, he gets into the chariot "to shed some of his golden feathers
there." At this, a voice from heaven laments, "My little ship, / O
what an ill-fated cargo you must bear!" (*Purgatorio* 32.124–129).
The eagle in the chariot symbolizes the Roman Empire entering
the church, but this great blessing to the church also brings temptation, preeminently the temptation of "golden feathers," the wealth
that the church enjoyed following the conversion of the Roman
Empire to Christianity. In particular, Dante may have in mind
the so-called "Donation of Constantine." According to the legend,
Constantine, the first Christian Emperor, was cured of leprosy by
the Roman bishop Sylvester, and out of gratitude he gave the whole
of the Western Empire to Sylvester and his successors. Throughout
the Middle Ages, this story was believed genuine, and it was used
by popes to bolster their claims to earthly power. Though Dante
probably thought it was genuine too, he clearly does not think it
was a good thing for the church. The "little ship" of the church was
not constructed to bear such "ill-fated cargo."[10]

Unable to bear golden feathers, the chariot begins to break up,
and as it does, "a dragon issued forth, / driving its tail up through

---

[10] In his treatise on politics, *Monarchia*, Dante laments the donation of Constantine
much as the heavenly voice does here: "O happy people, O glorious Ausonia [Italy], if only
that man [Constantine] who weakened your empire had never been born, or at least had
never been led astray by his own pious intentions" (II.xi.8; see Prue Shaw, trans. and ed.,
Dante, Monarchia (Cambridge: Cambridge University Press, 1995), 97.

the chariot." Using its "poison tail," the dragon tears "part of the floor" and then wanders away. Meanwhile, the chariot becomes overgrown with "thick weeds" (*Purgatorio* 32.130–141). The dragon no doubt refers to Satan, and the breaking up of the chariot pictures schism, the division of the church into warring factions. The first and greatest of the schisms occurred around 1054, when the Eastern and Western churches broke off communion in a cloud of mutual excommunications. Other divisions followed, with the result that the church, intended to be the new garden of God, became a weed-choked field.

The broken chariot begins "to sprout / heads from all parts: three on the chariot's pole / and one from each of its four corners grew" (*Purgatorio* 32.143–144). Three of the heads are "horned like oxen," but the four heads on the corners of the chariot have only one horn each (*Purgatorio* 32.145–147). It is as if the chariot itself is being transformed into a seven-headed beast, which is one of the images of Satan in Revelation (12:3). A total of ten horns protrude from the seven heads, another allusion to Revelation. The heads are also referring to the division of the papacy that occurred during the middle ages, when rival Popes would vie for "headship" in the church. For Dante, a chariot with several heads is nothing short of monstrous and diabolical.

Upon this monstrous chariot, Dante sees

> high on a hill, I saw an ungirt whore
> casting bold, sluttish glances all around.
> Acting as if someone might take her from him,
> A giant, I saw, standing there by her side;
> from time to time the two of them would kiss.
> But when she turned her roving, lustful eyes
> on me, her lover in a fit of rage
> beat her ferociously from head to foot.
> Then, furious with jealousy, the giant
> ripped loose the monster, dragging it away
> far off into the woods, until the trees
> blocked from my sight the whore and that strange beast.
> (*Purgatorio* 32.149–160)

Dante is again using imagery from the book of Revelation. The "ungirt whore" is the "whore of Babylon," who in Revelation 17:1–10 is seen riding on the back of a beast with seven heads and ten horns. In Revelation 17, the whore represents the city of Jerusalem, drunk with the blood of the saints, the "great city" where Jesus was crucified. Here in Dante, she represents a corrupted church, a church that has become an unfaithful bride instead of clinging to her husband. The giant is not from the book of Revelation and probably refers to the kings of France who during Dante's time were forming alliances with the papacy, manipulating the popes, and corrupting the church. Wanting the whore all to himself, the giant takes her and the chariot into the woods, a reference to the removal of the papacy to the French city of Avignon.

As the final canto of *Purgatorio* opens, nymphs are singing from Psalm 79, which laments the ruin of the Lord's temple and of Jerusalem. Perhaps those mournful lilies for Marcellus were appropriate after all. Ultimately, the lilies are not strewn for a funeral but as a promise of resurrection. As Beatrice goes on to assure Dante that the ruin of the church will not last forever, she reiterates the promise of a coming savior:

> The eagle that shed feathers on the car
>   that would become a monster, then a prey,
>   will not remain forever without heirs;
> I tell you this because I clearly see
>   those stars, already near, that will bring in
>   a time—its advent nothing can prevent—
> in which five hundred, ten, and five shall be
>   God's emissary, born to kill the giant
>   and the usurping whore with whom he sins.
>   (*Purgatorio* 33.37–45)

Beatrice knows that her prophecy is full of "dark words," but it is sufficiently clear to draw some conclusions. First, the giant-killer will come from the eagle that once occupied the chariot; it will be, in short, another Roman Emperor, if not a direct descendent of

REDEEMED FROM FIRE BY FIRE

Caesar. Second, the descendant from the eagle will kill the French "giant" and the whore; both the false church and the false state will be put down. Finally, Beatrice tells Dante to hope for a *cinquecento diece e cinque* (*Purgatorio* 33.43), a "five hundred, ten, and five," or 515. Dante is engaged in a complex plan on the 666 of Revelation 13:18, where that number stands as "the number of the beast." Instead of a bestial number, the 515 is the number of a deliverer. No one knows for sure whom Beatrice has in mind, but part of the answer may be that Beatrice intends for us to think of the number in Roman numerals: D = 500, X = 10, and V = 5. If these are arranged as DVX, the number spells out the Latin word *Dux*, which means "leader."[11] In any case, it seems clear that Dante's hope for the renewal of the church, while ultimately a hope in Christ, is also a hope for a political leader. The 515 is no doubt the same as the greyhound of *Inferno*, canto 1.

Like the parade, the vision of the transformation of the chariot has both historical and personal dimensions. It is not only an allegory of the history of the church, but also presents the climax of Dante's own transformation at the height of Purgatory. This becomes clear when we focus on the imagery of the tree in cantos 32 and 33. Dante has witnessed the resurrection of the tree of knowledge and fallen asleep under it, as the disciples fell asleep on the Mount of Transfiguration (*Purgatorio* 32.70–84). If the eagle represents Dante's own poetic "flight," then the damage the eagle does to the tree suggests that Dante himself has damaged the cause of the griffon with his waywardness. Because he has not been faithful to his beloved, his earlier work caused something like another fall from Paradise. Because his imagination and love have been transformed through the disciplines of Purgatory, however, he can put his past sins behind him and begin to soar again. So, at the end of the canto, Beatrice leads him to the source of the rivers of Eden, the Lethe and

---

[11] Mark Musa, *Dante's Purgatory* (Bloomington: Indiana University Press, 1981), 364, notes this "guess" and goes on to point out that many commentators link the "515" with Henry VII.

the Eunoe. Lethe removes memory of the past, but Eunoe renews memory of good deeds. Refreshed from these waters, Dante returns "reborn, a tree renewed, in bloom/ with new foliage, immaculate" (*Purgatorio* 33.143–144). He has become a fresh tree in the garden of Eden, the place where Adam began and where he fell because he ate from another tree. No longer another fallen Adam who damages the tree, he has become himself a mouthpiece for the "apple tree" that the angels crave to taste.

Being renewed as a tree of life is, however, just the beginning of the end. Getting back to the starting point is not the goal of the journey. Through the grace of Christ, mediated through the grace of Beatrice, Dante will ascend higher than Adam, beyond the tree, to the stars, and, even more, to the Love that moves them.

Review Questions

1. Describe the procession that Dante sees when he gets to the Garden of Eden.

2. What does the procession represent?

3. Who is the center of the parade?

4. Why does Beatrice rebuke Dante when she first sees him?

5. Explain the allegorical vision that Dante sees in the chariot.

6. What does Beatrice promise for the future?

7. What is the "515"?

Thought Questions

1. Virgil's last words to Dante are, "I crown and miter you lord of yourself" (*Purgatorio* 27.142). Where is Dante as he hears these words? How are the setting and the words connected?

2. Who is the young lady that Dante meets when he comes to the peak of Mount Purgatory? (*Purgatorio* 28.34–148; 33.119). What does she represent?

3. What does the lady sing? (*Purgatorio* 29.1–3) How is this related to Dante's experience in the Earthly Paradise, especially his baptisms in the two rivers?

4. Dante compares the chariot in the procession to the chariot of a Roman emperor and the chariot of the sun (*Purgatorio* 29.115–120). What is the significance of those comparisons?

5. What color are Beatrice's eyes? (*Purgatorio* 31.116) Why?

CHAPTER 5

JOIN THE DANCE
Paradiso

"I am not Aeneas; I am not Paul." These were the words that the pilgrim Dante, protesting like Moses, first spoke to Virgil when the Roman poet told him that he was to make a journey through the world of the dead. But the poem has shown Dante slowly being formed into an Aeneas and into a Paul. Like Aeneas, he has been learning the nature of true piety and true pity. In Purgatory, he has learned about defects and excesses of love in order to discover the nature of true Christian charity, which, according to Paul, is the greatest of Christian virtues (1 Cor. 13). In the final section of his journey, he is still acting as Aeneas and Paul. Aeneas journeyed from Troy to Rome, to a "home" that he had never visited before, and Dante's ascent to the presence of God is likewise a "homecoming." As he speeds through the spheres of Heaven, Beatrice assures him that "lightning / never sped downward from its home as quick / as you are now ascending to your own" (*Paradiso* 1.91–93). Aeneas, moreover, journeyed to the "Heaven" of the Greek underworld, the Elysian Fields, to meet his father, Anchises. Dante is also following the footsteps of Paul, being "caught up into Paradise" where he hears and sees "inexpressible words, which a man is not permitted to speak" (2 Cor. 12:4).

Though concerned with the completion of his training in love and piety, *Paradiso* begins with another motif from Dante's symphony. Virtually the first word of *Paradiso* is "glory," and this announces the theme of the whole canticle. The opening line speaks of the "glory of the One Who moves all things," the glory of the Creator and Ruler of the universe (*Paradiso* 1.1). But the original glory of God is not the sole focus of Dante's attention. This divine glory, he claims, "penetrates all the universe, reflecting / in one part more and in another less" (*Paradiso* 1.2–3). The glory of the Creator is manifested in every cranny of His creation, though not always in the same degree. Slugs and salamanders are glorious, but not so glorious as men or mountains.

Employing the image of light, Thomas Aquinas, the greatest of the medieval theologians, later explains more fully this view of created glory. Everything "which dies and all that cannot die / reflect[s] the radiance of that Idea which God the Father through His love begets" (*Paradiso* 13.52–54). By "Idea" Aquinas means the eternal Son of God, the Second Person of the Trinity, who became flesh in Jesus. He is the "Idea" of the Father, as He is the Father's Word, because in Him all the Father's mind is expressed. Aquinas also calls the Son the "Living Light," who "streams forth" from the Father. The Father is the "radiant Source" of the Light that is the Son, but the Light "never parts" from the "Source" that is the Father, nor from "the Love which tri-unites with them," that is, the Holy Spirit (*Paradiso* 13.55–57). The Father begets the Son through His love, and the Three Persons are united in the Love that is the Spirit. Radiant light and glory from the Son is a product of the Father's love for Him, and of the Spirit's loving work. Love and glory are closely linked in Dante's mind; though there can be glitz and glamour aplenty, without love there is no true glory. The glory that permeates the universe is specifically the glory of the Triune God, the God who is love. Dante will be a Paul only when he realizes that love has its source there, in the communion of Father, Son, and Spirit.

But the love-born glory of the Son is not the Son's alone. Rather, all created things reflect the "radiance" of the Son. This is so because the "Living Light" that is the Son "of Its own grace sends down its rays, as if / reflected, through the nine subsistencies / remaining sempiternally Itself" (*Paradiso* 13.58–60). The nine subsistencies may refer to the nine spheres of Paradise or to the nine orders of angels, but it does not really matter which. The Light of the Son is diffused as it moves from the higher reaches of the universe to the lower. Like a light penetrating water, it becomes dimmer at the lower end. Aquinas changes the picture to wax to explain further:

> The wax of things like these
> is more or less receptive, and the power
>   that shapes it, more or less effective—stamped
>   with the idea, it shines accordingly.
> So trees of the same species may produce
>   dissimilar fruit, some better and some worse;
>   so men are born with diverse natural gifts.
> And if the wax were perfectly disposed,
>   and if the heavens were at their highest power,
>   the brilliance of the seal would shine forth full;
> but Nature never can transmit this light
>   in its full force—much like the artisan
>   who knows his craft but has a trembling hand.
>   (*Paradiso* 13.66–78)

Aquinas gives two reasons why the natural world cannot manifest the complete radiance of God. The first has to do with the quality of the "wax" or the matter that is being formed to reflect the glory of the Son. Just as wax receives the imprint from a stamp, so the creation receives its "radiance" from the "imprint" of the Son's Light. But some wax is thicker and tougher to work, and in the same way it is harder to stamp the Son's glory on certain kinds of material. Dirt is harder to make luminous than the rainbow, or the emerald eyes of Beatrice. Secondly, the light from the heavens does not shine on the "wax" of creation with its full intensity. Earth cannot manifest that glory fully because the Son's glory is too "far away," and His Light has to pass through many layers before it reaches Earth. As Paul says, the glory of heaven differs from the glory of earth, and "there is one glory of the sun, and another glory of the moon, and another glory of the stars; for star differs from star in glory" (1 Cor. 15:41).

Aquinas is also explaining why creation is diverse, why there are so many different kinds of things and why they differ so much in quality. Different parts of creation reflect the Light of the Son in

different degrees. Though its parts display different degrees of glory,
all the diverse things of creation are ordered into a brilliant display
of beauty and light. The glory that Dante speaks of in the first line
of *Paradiso* is the glory of the "One Who moves all things." Just as
each thing reflects its particular degree of the Light of the Son, so
also everything moves toward the place that is appropriate to its
degree of glory.

In Paradise, the order of glory and light is not a hierarchy where
one thing is "higher" than another in glory. With a "hierarchy,"
everything is set in place and is supposed to stay in its place. It is an
immobile order, like the order of Hell. Heavenly order is an order
of coordinated movement in which things that differ in glory are
harmonized like notes of music or partners in a dance. This is a key
theme in the whole canticle, and it reflects Dante's Trinitarian belief
that the highest reality is the harmony of the different Persons of the
Trinity, and therefore this harmony is to be reflected in creation. In
particular, man is created to take a particular place in the dance of
the Heavens, as Beatrice shows in her answer to Dante's question
about "how I can rise through these light bodies here" (*Paradiso*
1.99). Beatrice explains that the order of all things "gives the form
that makes the universe resemble God" (*Paradiso* 1.104–105).
Rocks, which reflect God in a lesser degree than a man, are made
to be at a great distance from the Source of Light. Man's sin may
lead him down so that he ends up no better than a rock, and far
from the Light. Being endowed with intellect and the capacity for
love, however, man is made to go up. He is designed for a place in
Paradise, made to ascend, created to take his place in the dance.

Solomon explains the same dynamics more concisely and shows
the connections between glory and love:

> "Long as the joyous feast of Paradise
>   shall last," [he] said, "so long our burning love
>   shall clothe us in this radiance you see.
> Our brilliance is in ratio to our love,
>   our ardor to our vision, and our vision
>   to the degree of grace vouchsafed to us."
>   (*Paradiso* 14.35–42)

For Solomon, the radiance flowing from a man or woman is like the top story of a four-story house: Glory is built on love, which is built on vision, and the foundation of vision is a gift of grace.

The glory that shines forth from the Son draws out man's love. At the end of canto 4, Beatrice's eyes are shining with such great love and light that Dante is about to faint, and as canto 5 begins, she explains how she can be so transparent to the light of God:

> If, in the warmth of love, you see me glow
>> with light the world below has never seen,
>> stunning the power of your mortal sight,
> you should not be amazed, for it proceeds
>> from perfect vision which, the more it sees,
>> the more it moves to reach the good perceived.
> I can see how into your mind already
>> there shines Eternal Light which, of Itself,
>> once it is seen, forever kindles love;
> and should some other things seduce man's love,
>> It can be only some trace of this Light,
>> misapprehended, shining through that thing.
>> (*Paradiso* 5.1–12)

This important passage shows the connections between several of the key themes of *Paradiso* and of the *Comedy* as a whole. As we have seen above, God is the "Eternal Light" that shines in all creation, but only those who have "perfect vision" can see this Light in its true brightness. Seeing the Light "kindles love," and love makes the lover mobile. So he moves toward the Light, the good that is seen. This explains why Dante considers it so important to see things rightly. Creation has the capacity to "seduce" because it is filled with the Light of the Son. If one's vision is false, he will be drawn to love something that is not the true light, but only a dim mirror of the true Light. He will worship and serve the creature rather than the Creator. Having seen and loved falsely, he will be moved to act in a way that draws him toward the false light.

It is apparent, then, that the celestial dance is not only a harmony of persons with different degrees of glory; it also expresses love. Rivalry and competitiveness have no place in a dance. Each partner must yield to the other, seeking not to display his own skill but the combined skill of the dancers. The dance of glory is thus also a dance of love, and, like the dance of glory, its highest expression is the Trinity, the eternal *dance* of Father, Son, and Spirit, and the perfectly harmonized dance of God and man in the Incarnate Son.

Space Journey

C.S. Lewis summarized the medieval picture of "outer space" in this way:

> The central (and spherical) Earth is surrounded by a series of hollow and transparent globes, one above the other, and each of course larger than the one below. These are the "spheres," "heavens," or (sometimes) "elements." Fixed in each of the first seven spheres is one luminous body. Starting from Earth, the order is the Moon, Mercury, Venus, the Sun, Mars, Jupiter, and Saturn; the "seven planets." Beyond the sphere of Saturn is the *Stellatum*, to which belong all those stars that we still call "fixed" because their positions relative to one another are, unlike those of the planets, invariable. Beyond the *Stellatum* there is a sphere called the First Movable or *Primum Mobile*. This, since it carries no luminous body, gives no evidence of itself to our senses; its existence was inferred for the motions of all the others.[1]

Literally, *Paradiso* describes a space journey. Empowered by the power of Beatrice's eyes, Dante moves upward at tremendous speed through the nine spheres of heaven, and past the *Primum Mobile* to the highest heavens, which Dante calls the "Empyrean."

Like the other canticles, the journey through the nine spheres of Paradise is recounted in a three-part poem. The first three spheres

---

[1] *The Discarded Image: An Introduction to Medieval and Renaissance Literature* (Cambridge: Cambridge University Press, [1964] 1994), 96.

of Heaven, containing the Moon, Mercury, and Venus, are crossed by the shadow of Earth (cantos 1–9). This shadow symbolizes "defects" in the souls that are in these spheres, and the defects are symbolized by their positions in the heavens. Those who did not keep their vows are in the sphere of the moon, which is constantly changing its phases. Believers who acted to achieve fame are in the sphere of Mercury. Redeemed souls touched by lust are in the sphere of Venus, the planet bearing the name of the goddess of love. These defects are defects in the three "theological virtues" of faith, hope, and love. The chart below summarizes this section of *Paradiso*:

PLANET	DEFECT	CORRESPONDING VIRTUE	CANTOS
Moon	Inconstancy	Faith	2–4
Mercury	Ambition	Hope	5–7
Venus	Lust	Love	8–9

This initial section of the canticle is set off from the rest of *Paradiso* by the poet's intrusion at the beginning of canto 10. At the beginning of *Paradiso*, Dante had warned about the difficulty of the coming journey:

> I have been in His brightest shining heaven
> and seen such things that no man, once returned
> from there, has wit or skill to tell about;
> for when our intellect draws near its goal
> and fathoms to the depths of its desire,
> the memory is powerless to follow
> but still, as much of Heaven's holy realm
> as I could store and treasure in my mind
> shall now become the subject of my song.
> (*Paradiso* 1.4–12)

At the beginning of canto 10, as if he were beginning the canticle all over again, he speaks of the difficulty of describing what he has seen, and directly addresses the reader:

> Now, Reader, do not leave the table yet,
>   reflect upon what you have only tasted,
>   if you would dine on joy before you tire.
> I put the food out; now you feed yourself,
>   because the theme which makes of me its scribe
>   demands all of my concentration now.
>   (*Paradiso* 10.22–27)

Dante's second invocation and warning introduces a new section which covers cantos 10–30, and this large central section is
subdivided in two. First, there is a section that covers the four spheres
that contain the Sun, Mars, Jupiter, and Saturn. These planets correspond to the four natural virtues, each of which is represented by
a particular class of people:

PLANET	VIRTUE	REPRESENTATIVE	CANTOS
Sun	Prudence	Theologians	10–14
Mars	Courage	Soldiers	15–17
Jupiter	Justice	Rulers	18–20
Saturn	Temperance	Mystics	21–22

In each of these spheres, the blessed souls adopt some formation
that represents the virtue being revealed in the sphere. In the sphere
of the sun, Dante and Beatrice stand within the circumference of a
lovely double circle that spins around them. There is a Greek cross
on Mars, representing the martial spirit and the virtue of courage or
fortitude, and the souls form an eagle in the sphere of Jupiter, which
reminds us of the Roman eagle and the imperial justice associated
with it. Dante sees people going up and down a golden ladder in
the sphere of Saturn to symbolize contemplatives who ascend by
meditation into heavenly places.

After these four spheres, Dante crosses another threshold into
the sphere of the fixed stars (cantos 22–23). The passage to this
new section is not as obviously marked as some of the other major
transitions in the *Comedy*, but there are signs that the poet intended
to show this as the beginning of the climactic vision. Throughout

his journey, Dante has been following the footsteps of Jesus: he
entered Hell on Good Friday and spent time in Purgatory as Jesus
spent three days in the grave, and now as he enters the upper reaches
of Heaven, he sees Jesus' triumphant ascension, with Mary alongside
Him as *regina caeli*, the queen of heaven. Within the region of the
fixed stars, Dante focuses on the theological virtues rather than the
natural virtues. Peter, James, and John interrogate Dante on the
theological virtues of faith, hope, and love respectively.

Finally, Dante reaches the outer sphere of the physical Heavens,
the *Primum mobile* or "first mover," a moving sphere that causes
all the other spheres to move. There, he sees a point of light around
which nine lights whirl at supercelestial speed. These are the nine
orders of angels which whirl around the light of God, and this
nine-fold order of angels is the model of the nine spheres that he
has just passed through. Each sphere of Heaven thus corresponds
to one of the orders of angels. There are two indications that cantos
30–31 begins a new section. First, in canto 30, Dante bathes his
eyes in a stream of light, and once his eyes drink of the waters of
that stream, he sees the river of sparks and riverbank of flowers form
into the hosts of the elect, who take the shape of a rose. This is a
kind of baptism that corresponds to the baptism of fire by which
he entered the earthly paradise of Eden. Second, Beatrice leaves
off guiding the pilgrim; St. Bernard takes him up to the highest
Heaven instead.

Nine spheres of Heaven alert us to the parallels between
Paradise and the other regions of the world of the dead. But the
correspondences between the canticles go beyond the use of nine-
fold patterns. In each canticle, the first nine cantos are devoted to a
"preliminary" stage of the journey, and a major change takes place
in canto 9. After a long section, there is another major transition as
Dante reaches a climactic region. These parallels are summarized
in the chart on the next page.

The parallels among the canticles are sometimes quite exact,
even down to the placement of the cantos. Canto 6 of each canticle, for example, is devoted with political themes. In *Inferno*,

	INFERNO	PURGATORIO	PARADISO
9 cantos	before entry to Dis	before entry to purgatory	earth's shadow
central sections	circles of hell	terraces of purgatory	spheres of heaven
transition	well	passage through fire	"baptism" of eyes
climactic	Satan	Garden	Empyrean

Ciacco predicts some of the disasters that await Florence, a passage quoted in chapter one. This canto introduces the main political problem that concerns Dante: strife within Italy. Corresponding to this, canto 6 of *Purgatorio* expands on the problem with Dante's own diatribe against the corruption of Italy:

> Ah, slavish Italy, the home of grief,
>> ship without pilot caught in a raging storm,
>> no queen of provinces—whorehouse of shame! . . .
> O wretched Italy, search all your coasts,
>> probe to your very center: can you find
>> within you any part that is at peace?
>>> (*Purgatorio* 6.76–78, 85–87)

Though Dante commends the Roman Emperor Justinian for "repairing the bridle," his work has become useless since "the saddle's empty now." The only hope for Italy is that the church should "pursue your holiness" and allow "Caesar to take the saddle as he should" (*Purgatorio* 6.88–90, 93). Dante's wish for a restoration of the Justinian settlement is answered in *Paradiso*—and, significantly, in canto 6, which is given over entirely to Justinian.

Canto 15 is another example. In *Inferno* 15, Dante sees his old teacher, Brunetto Latini. Latini addresses him as a "son" (*Inferno* 15.31, 37) and predicts that Dante will suffer exile at the hands of the Florentines (*Inferno* 15.61–78). The scene with Latini is reminiscent of the scene in Virgil's *Aeneid* when Aeneas meets with his father Anchises in the underworld and is told of the future glories of Rome (Book 6). Latini is a father figure who predicts Dante's future, but that future is a bleak one. Latini, however, is in Hell, and he therefore is unable to play the role of Anchises to its fullest.

There is no corresponding scene in *Purgatorio* 15, but in *Paradiso* 15 and the following cantos, Dante meets Cacciaguida, his great-great grandfather and a Crusader. Cacciaguida remembers the glory of Florence before it exploded into factionalism:

> Florence, enclosed within her ancient walls
>   from which she still hears terce and nones ring out,
>   once lived in peace, a pure and temperate town:
> no necklace or tiara did she wear,
>   no lavish gowns or fancy belts that were
>   more striking than the woman they adorned.
> In those days fathers had no cause to fear
>   a daughter's birth: the marriageable age
>   was not too low, the dowry not too high.
> Houses too large to live in were not yet built,
>   and Sardanapalus had not yet come
>   to show to what use bedrooms can be put.
>   (*Paradiso* 15.97–108)

Rooted in the past as he is, Cacciaguida can also provide stable guidance for the future, and thus he can be a true Anchises to Dante's Aeneas. He does not ignore the exile that Dante will suffer, but, right at the center of *Paradiso*, he predicts that Dante's poem will become food for minds willing to listen:

> The conscience that is dark
>   with shame for his own deeds or for another's
>   may well, indeed, feel harshness in your words;
> nevertheless, do not resort to lies,
>   let what you write reveal all you have seen,
>   and let those men who itch scratch where it hurts.
> Though when your words are taken in at first
>   they may taste bitter, but once well-digested
>   they will become a vital nutriment.
> Your cry of words will do as does the wind
>   striking the hardest at the highest peaks,
>   and this will be for honor no small grounds;

and so you have been shown, here in these spheres,
> down on the Mount and in the pain-filled valley
> only those souls whose names are known to fame,
because the listener's mind will never trust
> or have faith in the kind of illustration
> based on the unfamiliar and obscure—
or demonstration that is not outstanding.

                                        (Paradiso 17.124–142)

Cacciaguida, the old Crusader, fires Dante up for a new crusade, a crusade fought with the weapons of words and truth, and *Paradiso* itself is the fulfillment of that prediction. Meeting his Anchises, Dante has become not only another Aeneas. He becomes another Virgil.

Review Questions

1. Explain the theology of "glory" that Aquinas talks about in canto 13.

2. How is glory related to love?

3. Discuss the symbolism of the "dance" in *Paradiso*.

4. What did medieval people believe about the structure of the solar system?

5. What do the first three spheres of Paradise have in common? Explain the structure of cantos 1–9.

6. What do the four planets in the second section of *Paradiso* represent?

7. What happens to Dante in the sphere of fixed stars?

8. What does Dante see in the *Primum Mobile*?

9. Explain the structural similarities in the three canticles of the *Comedy*.

10. Who is Cacciaguida? What is his role in the *Comedy*?

Thought Questions

1. Dante says that the sights he sees in Heaven are beyond any man's "wit or skill to tell about" (*Paradiso* 1.6). With whom is Dante comparing himself and his journey to Heaven? If no man can tell

about the things he sees, how can Dante tell about it? (*Paradiso* 1.22–27).

2. What is "Parnassus"? (*Paradiso* 1.17). Why does Dante mention it?

3. To what does Dante compare Heaven in *Paradiso* 1.79–81? In the light of the final cantos of *Inferno*, what is the significance of this comparison?

Shadow of the Earth: Cantos 1–9

The glory of the Son is symbolized by the light and glory of the sun. Neither can be looked at directly. In a profound simile, Dante notes how the sun "hides itself /within the very excess of its light" (*Paradiso* 5.134–135). We cannot look at the sun, but that is not because it is hidden; we cannot look at the sun because it is too bright. So also, the glory of the Son is diffused throughout the creation, manifested in everything that He has made. The Divine Light is not hard to see because it is veiled or hidden in some obscure corner of the universe. It is hard to see because we cannot look directly into the Light without going blind. We can begin to see the sun or the Son only when we have been given new eyes.

From the beginning of *Inferno*, Dante's goal has been to reach the sun. When he found himself lost in the Dark Wood, he began to climb a mountain where he saw the sun rising (*Inferno* 1.16–18). As he begins his ascent of Mount Purgatory, it is again to sunrise:

> The tender tint of orient sapphire,
> > suffusing the still reaches of the sky,
> > as far as the horizon deeply clear,
> renewed my eyes' delight, now that I found
> > myself free of the deathly atmosphere
> > that had weight heavy on my eyes and heart.
> The lovely planet kindling love in man
> > made all the eastern sky smile with her light,
> > veiling the Fish that shimmered in her train.
> > > (*Purgatorio* 1.13–21)

Again as he prepares to ascend to Paradise, he is considering the sun, "the lamp that lights the world" which "warms and seals/ the earthly wax closer to its own likeness" (*Paradiso* 1.37–42). And he is watching Beatrice stare at the sun, until the light that shines through her "poured through my eyes / into my mind and gave rise to my own: / I stared straight at the sun as no man could" (*Paradiso* 1.52–54). Gazing at the created sun that forms the "wax" of earth by lighting it, Dante prepares for a journey to the uncreated Sun who is the Living Light that lightens every man.

As noted above, the glory and light of the Son shine in different degrees in the creation. Every thing and every person has his particular degree of glory, and the degree of glory is determined by the will of God. But only sanctified men and women are content with God's ordering of things. This is the point made by Piccarda, whom Dante meets in the sphere of the moon. This is another case where a character in *Paradiso* answers the concerns raised in the earlier canticles. In *Inferno* 5, as we saw, Francesca talks at length of *amor*, love, and Dante is roused to pity for her. Though her speech is virtually a hymn to love, she is talking about adultery, and the talk of love covers over the grim reality of betrayal and murder. In *Paradiso* 3, Piccarda Donati tells the story of how she was forced to leave a convent and break her vows by being forced into marriage, and in doing so, Piccarda gives Dante's answer to Francesca. Unlike Francesca's "love," which led her to overreach her bounds, Piccarda speaks of a love that "tempers our will and makes us want no more / than what we have—we thirst for this alone" (*Paradiso* 3.70–72). Love occurs when a human will delights in the divine will. As she says in one of the most beautiful lines of the poem, "In His will is our peace" (*Paradiso* 3.85). In Piccarda, love and piety have kissed each other. In Piccarda, love means accepting one's assigned place in the dance of glory.

Piccarda's doctrine of love also addresses the issue of rewards and degrees of glory in heaven. Dante asks whether the souls that are in the lower spheres of Paradise long to move higher. She says that they do not, because the "essence of this blessed state / is to dwell here within His holy will, / so that there is no will but one with His" (*Paradiso* 3.79–81). This does not mean that everyone is equal in Heaven. Souls enjoy different degrees of blessedness. It is true that the souls are not really arranged as Dante sees them. As Beatrice explains,

> Not the most Godlike of the Seraphim,
>   not Moses, Samuel, whichever John
>   you choose—I tell you—not Mary herself
> has been assigned to any other heaven
>   than that of these shades you have just seen here,
>   and each one's bliss is equally eternal;
> all lend their beauty to the Highest Sphere,
>   sharing one same sweet life to the degree
>   that they feel the eternal breath of God.
>   (*Paradiso* 4.28–39)

There is only one Heaven, all heavenly happiness is eternal, and all souls in Paradise share the same life. In these respects, the souls are equal. But they share the same life in different degrees, depending on how strongly they "feel the eternal breath of God." What Dante sees in the nine spheres is not Heaven as it actually is; that vision will come only when he reaches the Empyrean and baptizes his eyes in a river of light. The nine spheres show heaven in a way that is accommodated to Dante's capacities. As a living man, he gains knowledge only through the five senses (*Paradiso* 4.41). If he were shown Heaven as it really is, he could not perceive it at all. To make Heaven accessible to his mind, God shows a "symbolic" vision that includes sights and sounds that do not really exist in Heaven. Like a parent speaking baby-talk to an infant, God bends low to speak to Dante in a way he can understand.

Piccarda is in the sphere of the moon, under the shadow of the earth, because she was forced to break her vow that she would never marry. Dante finds this unfair: "How can another's violent act / lessen the measure of my just deserts?" (*Paradiso* 4.20–21). Beatrice's answer is as follows: Suppose someone is forced to do something against his will. If he "gives in / even a little bit" to the force, then the person has contributed to the action and cannot be excused. Even if the person "fears" or "draws back," he has consented to the violence done to him. Piccarda could have "gone back into the cloister" after being forced into marriage, and since she did not, her faithfulness was found defective (*Paradiso* 4.79–81). When a person refuses to shrink back in the slightest degree, then he is completely a victim and cannot be blamed for the violence at all done to him. By way of contrast, Beatrice mentions Saint Lawrence, a Spanish martyr grilled alive because he refused to tell where church treasures were hidden. Lawrence did not fear, did not shrink back, and therefore his will remained intact. Unlike Piccarda, Lawrence showed no defect of faith.

When Dante and Beatrice ascend to the next sphere, they meet Justinian, the emperor of the Eastern Roman empire from 527 to 565, who was best known for codifying Roman law. Though he is in the sphere of Mercury, the place reserved for those who had an excessive love of fame, the canto in which he speaks focuses on the importance of the Roman empire in history. Justinian recounts the history of the "eagle," the emblem of Rome. Beginning with the story of Aeneas, Justinian traces the eagle's history through the time of the Republic, the Caesars, the fall of Rome, and into Dante's day. The greatest events of history were accomplished under the shadow of the eagle. When it accompanied Augustus, it "ushered in a world-wide peace" (*Paradiso* 6.80). God inspired the eagle to carry out the "glory of the vengeance of His wrath" when Jesus died on a Roman cross, and the same Justice "sped with Titus to avenge / the vengeance taken for the ancient sin" by destroying Jerusalem in A.D. 70 (*Paradiso* 6.88–93).

Justinian is, however, a figure of more than historical importance. He also sketches out Dante's own vision for a restored Roman empire. Justinian was a great emperor because he allowed himself to be directed in doctrine by the church. He was converted to the true faith by Agapetus, bishop of Rome. Once he was brought into conformity with true doctrine, "God in his grace inspired me to assume / that task to which I gave all of myself" (*Paradiso* 6.23–24). That task was not a military one but a legal one, the task of purifying "all the laws of excess and of shame" (*Paradiso* 6.12). Justinian thus represents the proper connection of church and state. The church concerns itself with right teaching, while the emperor, on the foundation of true doctrine, makes and enforces the civil laws of the empire. Justinian was "in step with Holy Church" (*Paradiso* 6.22). Dante implies that the earthly order should mimic the heavenly order. Peace and justice will exist on earth only if church and state act like partners in a dance, each accepting its role and each keeping in step with the other.

Justinian's discussion of the history of the eagle ends with a sharp condemnation of both the Guelfs and Ghibellines. The Guelfs had their own symbol, the yellow lily, while the Ghibellines claimed the Roman eagle as their own standard. Justinian berates the Ghibelline use of the eagle, since they have severed it from justice (*Paradiso* 6.103–105). As for the Guelfs, no one should think that "lilies can replace the bird of God" (*Paradiso* 6.111). Neither of the factions of fourteenth-century Italian politics can claim to be the heir of the Roman *imperium*, and only a revived empire can really hope to restore the eagle to its former glory.

One of the curious things about this canto is that Justinian, who is living in Paradise, is still deeply concerned with the course of events on earth. This is not an isolated example. Near the end of canto 9, Folquet of Marseilles, once bishop of Toulouse, launches a similar diatribe. At that point, Dante is in the sphere of Venus, the place reserved for those who were defective in love, and Folquet identifies one of the saints as Rahab, the harlot of Jericho. Mention of Joshua's conquest of Canaan reminds Folquet of the pope's indifference to the Holy Land, and the canto ends with a sharp polemic against the pope:

The Gospel and the fathers of the Church
   lie gathering dust, and Canon Law alone
   is studied, as the margins testify.

The Pope and Cardinals heed nothing else;
    their thoughts do not go out to Nazareth
    where Gabriel once opened wide his wings.
But Vatican and every sacred place
    in Rome which marked the burial-ground of saints
    who fought in Peter's army to the death,
shall soon be free of this adultery.
                    (*Paradiso* 9.133–142)

The Popes are condemned not only for neglecting the Holy
Land, but also for their adultery—a fitting discussion for the
sphere of Venus. But what is surprising is that there are any con-
demnations at all in Heaven, and even more surprising is that the
polemics get more intense as Dante ascends higher into Paradise.
Dante's vision of Paradise does not present souls enjoying a passive,
vacant bliss or sitting on clouds and strumming harps. Dante takes
God, and Heaven, too seriously for that kind of foolishness. Souls
in Paradise are close to God, and the more they see of His Light,
the more perfectly they love Him. For Dante, the converse is also
true: The more perfectly they love Him, the more fiercely they hate
everything that defaces His glory. The closer they get to God, the
more fully they can embrace the truth that Hell is a creation of
"primal love."

Review Questions

    1. What does the sun symbolize in the *Comedy*?

    2. Who is Piccarda? Why is she in the sphere of the moon?

    3. Are all souls in Heaven content with their place? Why or
why not?

    4. Are all souls in Heaven equally blessed?

    5. What is Justinian's discourse about in canto 6?

    6. How does Justinian express Dante's political outlook?

    7. Why are the saints in Heaven so severe with evils on Earth?

Thought Questions

1. What is Beatrice's explanation for the spots on the moon? (*Paradiso* 2.46–148).

2. What does Beatrice mean by two different types of "will"? (*Paradiso* 4.91–117).

3. Why does Beatrice say that a person who violates a vow cannot make up for it with other good deeds? (*Paradiso* 5.19–57).

4. What does Justinian say that puzzles Dante? (*Paradiso* 7.19–48).

5. How does Beatrice explain the necessity of the incarnation and death of Jesus? (*Paradiso* 7.58–120).

6. Charles Martel and Dante have a conversation about genetics. What is Martel's view? (*Paradiso* 8.94–148).

Twin Wheels of Holy Church: Cantos 10–14

Canto 10 marks the beginning of a new section of *Paradiso*, and like the first canto, it begins with consideration of the sun. Here, Dante's view of the sun is quite direct, for he has entered the sphere of the sun, the sphere that houses the souls of the prudent. That "fourth family" of God's children is kept "in constant bliss" because God shows "how He breathes, how he begets" (*Paradiso* 10.49–51). The "breathing" of God refers to the Spirit, and the "begetting" is the begetting by which the Father begets the Son. In the sphere of the sun, then, the prudent continuously see the glorious revelation of the Father's loving generation of the Son, and the Spirit's "tri-uniting" of the Three in One. The sun's glory is an image of the glory of the Trinity.

While Dante and Beatrice stand in the sphere of the sun, the prudent souls, each of them shining like a sun (*Paradiso* 10.76), circle three times around them, and then the voice of Thomas Aquinas begins to introduce others within the circle. Most are great theologians of the medieval church: Albertus Magnus, Thomas's teacher; Peter Lombard, whose *Sentences* was the most important textbook of theology; Dionysius, who wrote of the celestial spheres and of the orders of the angels; Boethius, a converted philosopher, famous for writing the *Consolation of Philosophy*; Isidore of Seville, who compiled a number of encyclopedia-like works; the Venerable Bede, historian of British Christianity and commentator on Scripture; and Richard of St. Victor, a mystical theologian. Solomon is there too, and "his flame contains that lofty mind instilled / with wisdom so profound—if truth speak truth— / there never arose a second with such vision" (*Paradiso* 10.112–114). After Thomas has introduced the members of the circle, he discerns that Dante has questions about things he has said. He had spoken of the road where the Dominican order of Friars are led as one "where all may fatten if they do not stray" (*Paradiso* 10.96), and then he pointed to Solomon as the wisest man that ever lived. Thomas proposes to explain these two statements (*Paradiso* 11.25–27), and the remainder of the cantos dealing with the sphere of the sun records the answers. The questions are answered according to the following outline:

> First discourse of Thomas: dealing with first question, canto 11
> Discourse of Bonaventure: dealing with first question, canto 12
> Second discourse by Thomas: dealing with second question, canto 13
> Solomon speaks, canto 14.1–75

There is also a neatly concentric structure in the first two discourses:

> Thomas introduces the members of the circle of souls
> Thomas's first discourse
> Bonaventure's discourse
> Bonaventure introduces the members of the second circle

Chiastic patterns appear a number of times in these cantos.[2] Canto 14 opens with Dante's description of the relation of Aquinas's words and Beatrice's, which are like "water in a round container"

---

[2] Rachel Jacoff, "An Introduction to *Paradiso*," in Rachel Jacoff, ed., *The Cambridge Companion to Dante* (Cambridge: Cambridge University Press, 1993), 214–215.

which "moves / center to rim rippling or rim to center" (*Paradiso* 14.1–2). This is a brilliant union of form and substance: Not only is line 2 written chiastically (center-rim-rim-center), but it is describing a circular movement. Like the line itself, the ripples move out and return to their origin. As Dante contemplates the whirling "reel" of the joyful souls, he hears them singing of "That One and Two and Three which never ends and ever reigns in Three and Two and One" (*Paradiso* 14.28–29). In this description, the Trinity itself forms a circle, a chiasm, as the Father begets the Son who sends the Spirit, who raises the Son to return to the Father.

Circular literary patterns are appropriate in this sphere which focuses on the two "wheels" of the church. In order to explain the first phrase, Thomas launches into a lengthy discussion of the two "guides" that God has given to assist the Bride of Christ on her pilgrimage toward "her Beloved." The first is resplendent with "seraphic love," while the second displays wisdom that shines with "a splendor of cherubic radiance." Though both are equally important for the guidance of the church, Thomas will speak of only one (*Paradiso* 11.28–42). Later, Bonaventure, a Franciscan friar who was leader of the order, describes the two as wheels of the "chariot that Holy Church used to defend herself / and conquer on the field of civil strife" (*Paradiso* 12.106–108). Without these two wheels, the chariot of Mother Church would be unable to conquer in the battle.

When Thomas gets around to telling about the first "wheel," it is a romance. The hero is a lover who, though only a youth, "braved his father's wrath" and was faithful in love to "a lady to whom all would bar their door as if to death itself." He took vows of marriage before a bishop and grew daily in love for her. This was no ordinary woman; she had once had a husband, but had been widowed for "eleven hundred years and more, / living without a lover till he came" (*Paradiso* 11.49–72). This, Thomas goes on to explain, is an allegory of the life of Francis of Assisi, the founder of the Franciscan order of friars, who were famous for their dedication to a life of simplicity and poverty and for their selfless ministry to the poor and outcasts. The lady is Poverty, and because of Francis's undying love for her, "their sweet accord, their faces spread with bliss, / the love, the mystery, their tender looks / gave rise in others' hearts to holy thoughts" and inspired others to make Poverty their lady (*Paradiso* 11.73–78).

For Dante, it is essential for the church as a whole to follow the program of Francis. When the church grows wealthy, she gets involved in worldly affairs and strays from her true spiritual mission. Frequent laments about the corrupting effects of wealth are scattered throughout *Paradiso*. Several cantos later, Peter Damian, a mystic and theologian, scorns wealthy church leaders in crude terms: "Your modern pastors need all kinds of help: / one here, one there, to lead, to prop and hold / up their behinds—they are so full of food; / their flowing cloaks cover the horse they ride: two beasts beneath one hide appear to move" (*Paradiso* 21.130–134). But the situation is more tragic still; not only has the church as a whole departed from Francis's Christlike example, but the Franciscans have as well:

> But his own flock is growing greedy now
> > for richer food, and in their hungry search
> > they stray to alien pastures carelessly;
> the farther off his sheep go wandering
> > from him in all directions, the less milk
> > they bring back when they come back to the fold.
> True, there are some who, fearing loss, will keep
> > close to their shepherd, but so few are these
> > it would not take much cloth to make their cowls.
> > > > (*Paradiso* 11.124–132)

This, Thomas concludes, is what he meant by talking about the road "where all may fatten if they do not go astray."

It is striking that Thomas should be the one to sing the praises of St. Francis, for he is a member of a rival order of friars, the Dominicans. His commendation of Francis is answered by a Franciscan, Bonaventure, who praises Dominic as Thomas has praised Francis. Where Francis devoted himself to the poor, Dominic was a "holy athlete, / kind to his own and ruthless to his foes" (*Paradiso* 12.56–57). As a young man, he had developed a "love of the eternal bread," became a theologian, and requested from the Pope "the right to fight the sinful world." Dominic became "a mighty torrent gushing from on high; / sending its crushing force against the barren / thickets of heresy, and where they were / toughest, it struck with the greatest violence" (*Paradiso* 12.84–85, 94–102). Like a new Adam, he was a "husbandman, the one chosen by Christ / to help Him in the garden of His Church" (*Paradiso* 12.71–72), and his torrential warfare against false teaching produced "other streams" that gave "their waters to the Catholic fields / so that its saplings might have greener life" (*Paradiso* 12.103–105). Through Dominic's preaching and teaching, weeds were pulled up from the garden of God, and the desert bloomed like the rose. Doubtless, Dante hopes that his poetry will be an equally productive "torrent of words."

Though as different as cherubim and seraphim, Dominic and Francis are as united as dance partners. Both "did battle for a single cause," and so closely allied are they in purpose that "their fame" shines "gloriously as one" (*Paradiso* 12.35–36). Both are "champions who through their words and deeds / helped reunite the scattered company" of the church (*Paradiso* 12.44–45). Most importantly, both are lovers. Francis was lover to the abandoned and ignored Lady Poverty, while Dominic was a "staunch lover of the Christian faith" (*Paradiso* 12.55). Francis is the courtly suitor, while Dominic is the chivalrous knight slaying dragons and delivering young damsels. Guided by these two, the church would have remained faithful and pure, and triumphant. The wheel of Francis would have led the church away from corrupting wealth, and the wheel of Dominic would have steered along the paths of truth.

Unfortunately, the wheel of Dominic has become as useless as the wheel of Francis:

> But now the track made by the topmost part
>   of that great wheel's circumference is gone,
>   and there is only mold where once was crust.
> His family, which once walked straight ahead

in his own footprints, now are so turned round
they walk along by putting toe to heel.
Soon comes the harvest time and we shall see
how bad the tillage was: the tares will mourn
That access to the storehouse is denied.

(*Paradiso* 12.112–120)

The "topmost part" of the wheel is Dominic himself, but the
wheel of the Dominican order no longer follows in the tracks their
founder made. Instead of weeding God's garden, the Dominicans
have become sowers of tares.

Thomas returns again in canto 13 to explain the second state-
ment that perplexes Dante. The question was how Thomas could
speak of Solomon as the wisest man, when Adam and Christ were
both apparently wiser.[3] Thomas concedes that Adam had a vision
of God that was clearer than any other man, because he had more
direct sight of God's Light. Before his sin, Eternal Light had perfectly
stamped its image on the "wax" of Adam. Yet, Solomon was still
the wisest man in his sphere: "when I talked of unmatched wisdom
then, / royal prudence was the wisdom upon which / I had my arrow
of intention drawn" (*Paradiso* 14.103–105). Solomon was not the
wisest man, but the wisest king.

In each of the spheres of natural virtue in cantos 10–30, Dante
sees the souls form some kind of figure that represents the teaching of that sphere. In the sphere of the sun, Dante first sees a circle
around himself and Beatrice, but after Aquinas has finished his first
discourse, he sees a double circle:

The very moment that the blessed flame
had come to speak its final word, the holy
millstone began revolving once again;

---

[3] Thomas describes Adam as that breast "from which was drawn the rib," and to Christ
as "That One Who pierced by the lance / gave satisfaction for future and past" (*Paradiso*
13.37–42). The parallel that he draws between the creation of Eve from Adam's rib and
the piercing of Jesus' side with the lance is a common one in medieval theology. Christ on
the cross is the new Adam, and the new Eve, the church, is formed by the blood and water
that flows from His pierced side.

before it could complete its first full round
    a second circle enclosing it:
    motion with motion, matching song with song—
Song that in those sweet instruments surpassed
    the best our Sirens or our Muses sing,
    as source of light outshines what it reflects.
As two concentric arcs of equal hue,
    are seen as they bend through the misty clouds
    when Juno tells her handmaid to appear—
The outer from the inner one an echo,
    like to the longing voice of her whom love
    consumed as morning sun consumes the dew—
and reassure the people here below
    that by the covenant God made with Noah,
    they have no need to fear another Flood—
even so those sempiternal roses wreathed
    twin garlands round us as the outer one
    was lovingly responding to the inner.
                    (*Paradiso* 12.1–21)

The second circle is also full of the souls of theologians, many of them Franciscans.[4] Double circles represent the two wheels of the Holy Church. Dante sees the wheels as they were meant to function. They "echo" one another, and each "lovingly responds" to the other. There is no hint of rivalry, but only of harmony and mutual support. Again, Dante hopes that the Church on earth will come to mirror the Heavenly wheels, for both "garlands" are necessary to crown and guide and beautify the Church, both the gentle love of Francis and the fierce love of Dominic.

Review Questions

    1. What saints are in the circles of the sphere of the sun?
    2. Explain the structure of cantos 11–14.

---

    [4]Dante also gets a brief glimpse of a third circle (*Paradiso* 14.73–75), but he is whisked away to the next sphere before he has a chance to fix his gaze on it.

3. Give some examples of "chiastic" or "concentric" patterns in this section. Why are they significant?

4. Who are the lovers in the romance that Thomas speaks of?

5. Why does Dante think St. Francis is so important?

6. How does Dante describe Dominic?

7. What has happened to the Franciscans and Dominicans?

8. What do the double circles represent?

Thought Questions

1. To what does Dante compare the souls in the sphere of the sun? (*Paradiso* 10.91–93). Why is this significant?

2. What is Dante talking about at the beginning of canto 11? How does it reflect his setting in Paradise?

3. Dante says that Francis's hometown is best called "Orient" (*Paradiso* 11.54). Why?

4. Identify two of the souls in the second circle (*Paradiso* 12.127–145).

5. Why does Aquinas tell Dante to weigh down his feet with "leaden weight"? (*Paradiso* 13.112–117). What kind of weight is he talking about?

Love Justice: Cantos 18–21

A double circle is appropriate to the themes of the sphere of the sun, but it plays little part in the action that occurs in that sphere. The same cannot be said of the image that forms when Dante enters the sphere of Jupiter, the sphere of justice. Like a celestial marching band, the souls parade around and form a Latin inscription, which reads, "*Diligite justitiam qui judicatis terram.*" These words, which form the opening verse to the apocryphal book, the Wisdom of Solomon, mean "Love justice, you who judge on the earth." After they have formed the inscription, the final M in "*terram*" begins to change until Dante sees "the crest and neck of a great eagle" (*Paradiso* 18.107–108). The beak of the eagle's head begins to move, and the eagle speaks to Dante about justice.

The eagle is a significant image on a number of levels. In *Paradiso* 6, Dante has heard Justinian discourse at length about the history of the eagle, the emblem of the Roman world. Here, the eagle is an image of heavenly justice, but "justice on earth/ comes from that Heaven which you yourself begem" (*Paradiso* 18.116–117). Heavenly justice is the model for earthly justice, and just as heavenly justice is revealed in the pattern of the eagle, so the history of the Roman eagle is the history of justice on earth. It is no accident that the Roman eagle forms from the last letter of *terram*. For Dante, the world would be a better place if *terram* and eagle were indeed one.

In Dante's political writings, he argued that power is best located in one person. It would be no improvement for a Roman bureaucracy to rule the world since that bureaucracy would split up into factions, just as Europe, and especially Italy, had been split apart. Justice demands an emperor, a beneficent tyrant who has all earthly power in his hands. The heavenly eagle represents this theory. When it begins to speak, Dante "heard its voice use words like I and Mine / when in conception it was We and Ours" (*Paradiso* 19.11–12). Because the eagle was made up of many souls, it would have been appropriate to use the plural, but these many are united in one "I" and "Mine" and "Me," just as the many peoples and nations of the Roman empire are embodied in its emperor.

Since it has the benefit of Scripture and the Church, Christendom should excel all other nations in justice. But the reality is far otherwise. Canto 19 ends with a litany of conflicts, wars, and other injustices that plague Christian Europe, evils that are so great that even pagan Ethiopians and Persians will stand appalled at the last judgment. Among the conflicts, Dante mentions the "thirsting pride / by which the Scot and Englishman are maddened, / neither content to stay within his bounds" (*Paradiso* 19.121–123). Dante is referring to the wars between Edward I of England and the Scottish bands led by William Wallace and Robert the Bruce. Had he

lived to see *Braveheart*, Dante would not have been cheering for
Mel Gibson.

The eagle's speech is not only concerned with political justice.
In fact, before he begins to speak, Dante speaks about justice and
injustice in the Church. Issues of justice in Church and state are
woven throughout these cantos with questions concerning the justice
of God, which lead into considerations of God's sovereign will and
predestination. There are four main sections:

> Injustice in the Church (Dante)
> Justice of God (Eagle)
> Injustice in the political realm (Eagle)
> Justice of God (Eagle)

Injustice in the Church is the initial theme. As Dante stands
awestruck at the eagle of justice, he begins to pray that God would
"examine / the place whence comes the smoke that dims your rays"
(*Paradiso* 18.119–120). The rays are the rays of justice, and the
place that produces the smoke is evidently the Church, for he goes
on to pray that God's wrath would "descend upon, once more / all
those who buy and sell within the temple / whose walls were built
with miracles and martyrs" (*Paradiso* 18.121–123). Dante is again
attacking the wealth of the Church, its failure to follow the path set
by Francis, a failure that sends up clouds of corruption that obscure
justice.

In addition to the corruptions that come with material wealth,
the Church is a place of injustice because it wages war not with
swords but by "withholding here and there / the bread our Father's
love denies to none" (*Paradiso* 18.128–129). Instead of offering the
bread of communion to all Christians, the Church uses the threat
of excommunication for blackmail and manipulation. In fact, some
Popes used excommunication as a way of generating income. They
imposed the sentence of excommunication and then promised to
rescind it, for a price. Thus, the injustice of the Church's wealth
and her unjust use of the Lord's bread are connected. Withholding the Lord's bread for profit is one of the symptoms of church

leaders being more intent on feeding their bellies than on feeding the poor. Another dimension to the combination of I and We in the celestial eagle emerges here: Heavenly justice is mirrored on earth when goods are joined together as "ours" and when the goals and purposes of the many are coordinated and harmonized into one. Justice on earth should reflect the reality of heaven, which rings with "a single sound composed of many loves" (*Paradiso* 19.21). Especially in the Church, the many should act for the common good. The many members should act as one, for they all partake of one bread.

The eagle's first speech is concerned with divine justice. God the Judge is also God the Creator, and creation is an act of justice because when God made the world, "His compass drew / the limits of the world and out of chaos / brought order to things hidden and revealed" (*Paradiso* 19.40–42). Order and justice are closely connected in Dante's mind, and God's ordering of the world, His placement of everything, reflects His eternal justice. He has given everything exactly the place, power, and purpose that is fitting. Each thing has just the right degree of glory, its rightful place in the dance.

This does not mean, however, that the justice of God is readily apparent to men. On the contrary, looking into the justice of God is like trying to peer to the ocean floor:

> while you can see the bottom near the shore,
> you cannot out at sea; but nonetheless
> it is still there, concealed by depths too deep.
> There is no light except from the clear sky
> forever cloudless—darkness is the rest,
> the shadow or the poison of the flesh.
> (*Paradiso* 19.61–66)

Dante's notion of the incomprehensibility of God's justice is linked to his theology of glory and light. The Light of the Word impresses itself on creation, but even when the creation has reflected as much Light as it possibly can, the Word is still infinitely brighter.

Our vision is only "one of the rays that come from the prime Mind," and therefore he has to conclude that "its own Principle / is far beyond what our eyes can perceive" (*Paradiso* 19.43–57). Our grasp of God's justice, like our reflection of His glory, is only in degree and never in full.

Righteous pagans pose a challenge to God's justice. Imagine a man of good desires and good actions, who never sins at all, yet dies "unbaptized, dies without the faith." Why is such a man condemned? How can it be his fault that he did not turn to Christ? The eagle's first response to this is Pauline through and through:

> Now who are you to sit in judgment's seat
> 　　and pass on things a thousand miles away,
> 　　when you can hardly see beyond your nose? . . .
> O earthbound creatures! O thick-headed men!
> 　　The Primal Will, which of Itself is good,
> 　　never moves from Itself, the Good Supreme.
> 　　　　　　　　　　　　　(*Paradiso* 19.79–87)

The eagle has apparently been reading Romans: "Who are you, O man, who answers back to God? Shall the thing formed say to Him who formed it, why did you make me like this?" (Rom. 9:20). But Dante is doing more than appealing to the sovereign power and will of God. He is also saying that whatever God does with his creation is good, because God is the "Good Supreme." What makes Dante confident that God acts justly toward pagans is His confidence that God is always just. In addition to this, the eagle also points out that those who lack faith will not be the furthest from God. Though only believers will enjoy the delights of Paradise, people who falsely profess Christ "will be less close / to Him than will those who know not Christ" (*Paradiso* 19.107–108). Hypocrites will be punished more severely than ignorant pagans. Limbo is not Paradise, but it is far better than Malebolgia.

A similar issue is handled in a somewhat different way in the following canto. The eagle directs Dante's attention to his eye and eyebrow. At the center of the eye is the king who "wrote songs inspired by the Holy Spirit," that is, David. The eyebrow is made up of five other rulers, among them Trajan, the Roman Emperor, and Ripheus, a Trojan hero who fell when the Greeks took the city and who was known as the most just of the Trojans. Dante is puzzled that two pagans should be so prominent in the eagle of justice, especially since the eagle has already told him that "to this realm / none ever rose who had not faith in Christ,/ before or after he was crucified" (*Paradiso* 19.103–105). The eagle explains that these two "did not leave their bodies, as you think, / as pagans, but as Christians with firm faith" (*Paradiso* 20.103–104). In reward for his virtue, Trajan was returned "back to his flesh and bones" and during the short additional life he believed on "Him Who had the power to save." Ripheus, who lived before the coming of Christ, had his eyes opened by grace to see the truth. Long before baptism was instituted, he was baptized by faith, hope, and love (*Paradiso* 20.106–129).

Ultimately, the fate of man rests with God's will and not man's. He determines who is saved and who is not:

> Predestination! Oh, how deeply hid
> > your roots are from the vision of all those
> > who cannot see the Primal Cause entire!
> You men who live on earth, be slow to judge,
> > for even we who see God face to face
> > still do not know the list of His elect,
> but we find this defect of ours a joy,
> > since in this good perfected is our good;
> > for whatsoever God wills we will too.
> > > > (*Paradiso* 20.130–138)

Predestination is reiterated by the mystic Peter Damian in the next sphere of heaven, the sphere of Saturn. Here dwell the contemplatives, those who meditate on God in order to know Him as intimately as possible. Damian, mystic that he is, knows that there are limits that humans will never cross. Dante asks why only Damian has been given his particular calling, and Damian answers by appealing to God's sovereign good pleasure. Each soul has a particular task assigned by "that deep charity which urges us/ to serve the wisdom governing the world" (*Paradiso* 21.70–72). To some extent, this divine wisdom can be known by man, for Damian himself shines with particular brightness because of the "clarity of spiritual vision." No matter how illumined a human soul becomes, however, no one can penetrate the plan of God: "The truth you seek to fathom lies so deep / in the abyss of the eternal law, / it is cut off from every creature's sight" (*Paradiso* 21.94–96). Man must simply bow before His greatness, for "in His will is our peace."

Review Questions

1. What inscription do the souls in the sphere of Jupiter form?
2. What does the "M" form? Why is this symbol significant?
3. What forms of injustice does Dante see in the church?
4. How is creation a just act?
5. To what does the eagle compare the justice of God? What does that comparison mean?
6. How does the eagle defend God's justice in the case of the righteous pagan?
7. Whom does Dante see in the eyebrow of the eagle? Why is this odd?
8. How does the eagle answer Dante's questions about the saints in the eyebrow?

Thought Questions

1. What does Cacciaguida tell Dante about his great-grandfather? (*Paradiso* 15.91–96). What is Dante supposed to do with that information?
2. What does Dante say about nobility at the beginning of canto 16?
3. Is Dante a Calvinist? Look especially at *Paradiso* 17.37–42.
4. To what does Cacciaguida compare Heaven in *Paradiso*

18.28–36? How is this connected to earlier uses of the same imagery?

5. What is Dante's relation to the eagle of justice in *Paradiso* 19.91–96? What does this suggest about Dante's view of his own calling?

6. How does Dante define "love entirely free" in *Paradiso* 21.73–75? How does this connect to the theme of freedom in other parts of the *Comedy*?

7. What are the saints shouting about at the beginning of canto 22? What does this tell us about Heaven?

8. What has happened to the Benedictine order of monks? (*Paradiso* 22.70–96).

The Greatest of These: Cantos 24–33

Prudence, Courage, Justice, and Temperance are genuine virtues, but they do not rise to the level of the theological virtues of faith, hope, and love. While Aristotle would cite justice as the leading virtue, Dante believes, with Paul, that charity or love is the "greatest of these." As he rises above the spheres of the planets into the sphere of the fixed stars, Dante is rising beyond the merely natural virtues to distinctly Christian virtues. There he is quizzed by three apostles, Peter, James, and John, concerning faith, hope, and love. In each case, the apostle asks for a definition of the particular virtue and then poses further questions. And in each case, Dante himself is asked whether he has gained possession of these qualities.

Questioned by Peter about faith, Dante replies with a quotation from Hebrews 11: "Faith is the substance of those hoped-for things / and argument for things we have not seen" (*Paradiso* 24.64–65). Peter agrees but presses for definitions of "substance" and "argument." Dante's answer is that faith provides the foundation or basis for hope, and therefore it can be called a "substance," which literally refers to something "standing under" another thing. Faith is an argument because "from this belief we must construct / logical proofs for what cannot be seen" (*Paradiso* 24.76–77). Dante does not believe that logic and reason function by themselves, but within the circle of faith, they have their place. When Dante confesses that his faith rests on the "bountiful / rain of the Holy Spirit showering / the parchments, Old and New," Peter asks how he knows that the Scriptures teach the truth. His answer is revealing: "The proof that what I read is true / is in the works that followed: Nature's hand / could never heat or forge that kind of iron" (*Paradiso* 24.100–102). Scripture is proved true not when one makes a good argument, but when one lives in obedience to what Scripture teaches. Since the teachings of Scripture run so counter to our natural inclinations, when they are obeyed it is a miracle beyond all possible miracles. That proves Scripture bears the power of God.

Having graduated from the school of faith, Dante moves on to be questioned by James about hope. Hope, he declares, "is sure expectancy of future bliss / to be inherited—the holy fruit / of God's own grace and man's precedent worth" (*Paradiso* 25.67–69). Like faith, hope is a response to the word of God, which "defines the goal" and "points me to the promise" (*Paradiso* 25.88–90).

Love is the culmination of Dante's education, and it is the apostle John, the "beloved disciple," who quizzes him on this virtue. Here again Dante's theology of glory is brought out. God, as the true Good, is the goal of all human seeking. Dante has come to know and seek the Good through the persuasiveness of "philosophic arguments" and also by the "authority" of Scripture and the Church. Once perceived as good, the Good "enkindles love, / and makes that love more bright the more that we / can comprehend the good which it contains" (*Paradiso* 26.25–30). Once drawn out by the goodness of God, love expands to encompass the whole creation:

> The being of the world and my own being,
> the death He died so that my soul might live,
> the hope of all the faithful, and mine too,

joined with the living truth mentioned before,
    from that deep sea of false love rescued me
    and set me on the right shore of true Love.
I love each leaf with which enleaved is all
    the garden of the Eternal Gardener
    in measure of the light he sheds on each.
                        (*Paradiso* 26.58–66)

God's love, manifested in Christ's death, drew Dante away from false loves. Ultimately, though, love for God does not draw us away from love of the world; rather, love of God flows out in love of the world that manifests His Light. In this Light, the world becomes an Eden, and each leaf an object of love.

After his catechism class, Dante moves from the heaven of fixed stars to the *Primum Mobile*. This sphere contains no souls of the dead and no planet, and it represents no particular kind of virtue. Instead, it serves a purely mechanical purpose. Unlike the other spheres, which derive their movement from the spheres outside, the *Primum Mobile* is moved by "no other sphere," but instead "all the others measure theirs by this" (*Paradiso* 27.115–117). In the *Primum Mobile*, however, Dante is able to see the model of the created heavens: A point of light so bright that no eyes could look at it, which is circled by nine "rings of fire" moving at a speed that no sphere of Heaven could match (*Paradiso* 28.16–36). The light at the center is the light of God Himself, and He is encircled by the nine orders of angels.

One thing puzzles Dante about the vision that he sees in the *Primum Mobile*. In that model, the sphere closest to the center, which is smallest, moves at the highest speed. By contrast, in the physical universe, the spheres that are largest and furthest from earth move at the highest speeds. The model and the copy seem to be opposites. Beatrice explains that the issue does not have to do with the circumference of the spheres, but with the power, and the power of a particular sphere depends on how close it is to God. Thus, the closest sphere to the point of light corresponds to the *Primum Mobile*, and the sphere furthest from the point is the sphere of the moon. What Dante is expressing here is a key point of the medieval view of the world. Though they believed that the earth was the center of the created universe, in another sense, it was on the outside, and the center was in God. In this sense, earth stands at the furthest edge of the universe. As C.S. Lewis put it, we gaze at the stars and think we are looking *out*; the medieval would gaze at the stars and think he was looking *in*.[5]

Even when he has seen the model in the *Primum Mobile*, Dante has not yet had a clear vision of how Heaven is really constructed. That vision can come to him only after he comes to a "flowing stream" of light and drinks the waters (*Paradiso* 30.61–74). Immediately he begins to see Heaven as it truly is:

> before my eyes the sparks and flowers changed
> > into a greater festival: I saw
> > both courts of Heaven in their reality. . . .
> There is a light above whose glory makes
> > Creator visible to his creations
> > whose only peace is in beholding Him;
> in figure of a circle this light spreads,
> > and is so vast that its circumference
> > would be too loose a belt to bind the sun.
> And its expanse comes from a single ray
> > striking the summit of the First Moved Sphere
> > from which it takes its vital force and power.
> And as a hillside rich in grass and flowers
> > looks down into a lake as if it were
> > admiring the reflection of its wealth,
> so mirrored, tier on tier, within that light,
> > more than a thousand were reflected there,
> > I saw all those of us who won return.
>
> > > > (*Paradiso* 30.94–114)

---

[5] Lewis, *Discarded Image*, 118–119.

Heaven is now revealed not as a series of spheres but as a white Rose whose petals consist of the saints who are gathered around the throne of God.

By this time Beatrice has left him, replaced by St. Bernard (*Paradiso* 31.58-63), abbot of Clairvaux and author of works of theology, mysticism, and many hymns. Bernard explains the arrangement of the saints in the Empyrean. Top and center in the Rose is Mary, and the great women of the Bible are nearby: Eve, Rachel (with Beatrice just to her side), Sarah, Rebecca, Judith, and Ruth. At the opposite side of the rose are great men, including John the Baptist, Francis, Benedict, and Augustine. On either side of Mary are

> Those two who sit most blest in their high thrones
>> because they are closest to the Empress
>> are, as it were, the two roots of our Rose:
> he, sitting on her left side, is that father,
>> the one through whose presumptuous appetite
>> mankind still tastes the bitterness of shame;
> and on her right, you see the venerable
>> Father of Holy Church to whom Christ gave
> the keys to this beautiful Rose of joy.
>> (*Paradiso* 32.118–126)

These roots are Peter and Adam, the father of the race and the father of the Church. A vertical line divides the rose between those who lived and believed before Jesus came and those who lived during and after His life, death, and resurrection.

The Rose is constantly "pollinated" by angels who "like bees . . . descended all at once on that great bloom / of precious petals, and then flew back up / to where its source of love forever dwells" (*Paradiso* 31.7–12). As they move back and forth, the angels "spread the peace and ardor of the love / they gathered with their wings in flight to Him" (*Paradiso* 31.17–18). Even the angelic flights pose no obstacle to the light of God, which bathes the whole Rose in glory. Dante has been traveling since the beginning to see such

Light, such Love, such beauteous harmony.

Nevertheless, even the Rose of the Empyrean is not yet the end of the journey. He has not come through Hell and Purgatory only to see the saved; he hopes to see the Savior. He will not be satisfied to see those who are loved and who love; he desires to see Love. That love is revealed as a Trinity, a "Great Light" that shines in three circles in three clear colors bound in one same space;

> the first seemed to reflect the next like rainbow
> on rainbow, and the third was like a flame
> equally breathed forth by the other two.
> (*Paradiso* 33.116–120)

The Father's circle is reflected, "like rainbow on rainbow," in the Son, and the Spirit is "breathed forth" from both together. In the height of his ecstasy, Dante sees at the heart of the Trinity a vision that defies reason. As he looks at the "first reflected light" from God, that is, the Son, it begins to take on "man's very image." This, it appears, is not something added to the Light; rather, it is in man's very image "in Itself and in Its own Self-color" (*Paradiso* 33.127–132). Humanity is not something extraneous to the Light that is the Son, but rather it reveals the true nature of the Son. Here is the highest expression of love, the self-condescending love that sends Beatrice to aid a pilgrim lost in a dark wood, the terrifying love that constructed Hell, the fiery love that keeps alive the flames of Purgatory; above all, it is the love of a God who did not think equality with God was something to be grasped, but humbled Himself to take on the form of a servant.

Paradiso is full of circles and is itself a circle, ending where it began, with the glory and love of the one who "moves" all things (*Paradiso* 1.1; 33.145). *Paradiso* also ends where the other canticles have ended. As Dante and Virgil emerged from Hell, they "came out to see once more the stars" (*Inferno* 34.139), and *Purgatorio* closes with Dante renewed and "eager to rise, now ready for the stars" (*Purgatorio* 33.145). These endings give a small taste of the final ending that is yet to come. But Dante rises even higher than he anticipates. He has not finished his course when he has reached the sphere of fixed stars, or the Empyrean. He does not leave off with the stars but ascends to the Love that moves them, to the vision of the Triune God. It is the vision of the Father's love for the Son that shines throughout the creation, and preeminently of God as Incarnate Love.

When he sees that, he can go no higher. He has completed his ascent to love. And there is nothing else to do other than take his predestined place in the dance, turning in perfect balance like the wheeling stars moved by Love Divine.

Review Questions

1. Whom does Dante meet in the circle of the fixed stars?
2. How does Dante answer Peter's questions about faith?
3. How does he answer John's questions about love?
4. In Dante's view, does love for God pull us away from love of the world? Why or why not?
5. What is the function of the *Primum Mobile*?
6. Why is Dante puzzled by the vision he sees in the *Primum Mobile*? How does Beatrice explain it?
7. What do the saints look like in the Empyrean?
8. What is the ultimate vision that Dante sees?

Thought Questions

1. To what does Dante compare faith? (*Paradiso* 4.115–117). What is the point of the comparison?
2. What does Dante hope for at the beginning of canto 25? What will help him achieve that hope?
3. Who is the "Pelican" in *Paradiso* 25.112–114? Why is he being compared to a Pelican?
4. What questions does Dante ask of Adam? (*Paradiso* 26.91–142). What are Adam's answers?
5. Why did God create the world? (*Paradiso* 29.10–36). What does Beatrice mean by a "threefold creation"? (*Paradiso* 29.28).
6. What accounts for the different ranks of the Empyrean? (*Paradiso* 32.72–75).

AUTHOR INDEX

A

B

C

D

E

F

Warren — Hauh

soaring poetic gifts

CPSIA information can be obtained
at www.ICGtesting.com
Printed in the USA
FSOW04n1016120515
6995FS

9 781885 767165